Contents

KU-779-490

Introduction

Welcome to the new edition of **Talk Mandarin Chinese**, BBC Active's course for absolute beginners, which has already inspired and helped so many people to learn Chinese from scratch and given them the confidence to have a go.

The key to **Talk Mandarin Chinese**'s effectiveness is the successful **Talk** method, developed by experienced teachers of languages to adult beginners. Its structured and systematic approach encourages you to make genuine progress and promotes a real sense of achievement.

The choice of situations and vocabulary is based on the everyday needs of people travelling to China. The language is presented using *pinyin*, the official Chinese system of using Roman script, i.e. the same alphabet as English, to represent the sounds of Chinese.

Talk Mandarin Chinese introduces some basic Chinese characters but the main emphasis is on talking and listening. The course includes 120 minutes of recordings of Chinese native speakers.

> Wherever you see this: **1•5**, it means that the phrases or dialogues are on the CD (i.e. CD1, track 5).

The book in this new edition has several additional features, inspired by feedback from users and teachers. It includes a two-way glossary (pages 133–144), covering around 1,000 words, and the popular **Talk** *Wordpower* (pages 128–130), designed to increase your vocabulary fast.

There's also a free video-based course on the BBC website: www.bbc.co.uk/languages/chinese/real_chinese/. This covers similar content at the same level, providing additional exposure and reinforcing the language against the background of Chinese culture. Free tutors' support and activities for use in the classroom are available online at www.bbcactivelanguages.com.

Acknowledgements

BBC Active would like to thank everyone who contributed to this course. Our particular thanks go to Kan Qian, Dr Yu Hong Zhang, Wang Xiaoning, Li-yun Liao and Liu Chang.

Z957934

BBC

| TALK |

Mandarin
Chinese

YU FEIXIA &
ALWENA LAMPING
Series Editor: Alwena Lamping

BBC Active, an imprint of Educational Publishers LLP, part of the Pearson Education Group, Edinburgh Gate, Harlow, Essex CM20 2JE, England

© Educational Publishers LLP 2015

BBC logo © BBC 1996. BBC and BBC ACTIVE are trademarks of the British Broadcasting Corporation.

First published 2008.
Second edition 2015.
5 4 3 2 1

ISBN 978-1-4066-8007-2

Cover design: Two Associates
Cover photograph: © iStock/yuji
Insides design: Nicolle Thomas, Rob Lian
Layout: DTP Media Ltd. www.dtp-media.co.uk
Illustrations © Tim Marrs @ Central Illustration Agency
Publisher: Debbie Marshall
Development editor: Kan Qian
Project editor: Emma Brown

Audio producer: Martin Williamson, Prolingua Productions
Sound engineer: Katy Brier and Paul Kirkin at The Audio Workshop
Presenters: Sun Chen, Wang Xiaoning, Chuanzi Xing, Howard Zhang

Printed in China (CTPSC/1).

The Publisher's policy is to use paper manufactured from sustainable forests.

Making the most of Talk Mandarin Chinese

1 Read the first page of the unit to focus on what you're going to learn and set it in context. Then follow steps 2 to 5 for each of the next four pages.

2 Listen to the key words and phrases – don't be tempted to look at them first. Then listen to them again, this time reading the *pinyin* version in your book too. Finally, try reading them out loud before listening one more time.

3 Work your way through the activities on the page. These highlight key language elements and are carefully designed to develop your listening skills and your understanding of Chinese. The pace of these dialogues deliberately avoids being over-slow, which can lead to false expectations – so each activity has its own track so that you can listen to it several times. The *Answers* section starts on page 99.

4 Read the **Zài Zhōngwén lǐ** explanations of how Mandarin Chinese works as you come to them – they're placed just where you need that information. The symbol G12 means that there's further explanation in the *Grammar* section.

5 After completing the activities, and before you try the *Put it all together* page, close your book and listen to the conversations straight through. The more times you listen, the more familiar Chinese will become and the more comfortable you'll become with it. You might also like to read the dialogues at this stage – preferably out loud (*Transcripts*, starting on page 99).

6 Complete the consolidation activities in *Put it all together* and check your answers (starting on page 99).

7 Use what you have just learnt – the native speaker presenters on the audio will prompt you and guide you through the *Now you're talking* page as you practise speaking Mandarin Chinese.

8 Check your progress. First, test your knowledge with the *Quiz*. Then see if you can do everything on the checklist – if in doubt, go back and spend some more time on the relevant section. You'll have further opportunities to check your progress in the strategic *Checkpoints* after Units 4, 7 and 10.

9 Read the learning hint at the end of the unit, which offers ideas for consolidating and extending what you've learnt.

10 Finally, relax and listen to the whole unit, understanding what the people are saying in Chinese and taking part in the conversations. This time you may not need the book to hand.

Pronunciation guide

1   Most consonants sound broadly similar in *pinyin* and English, except for the following, which sound approximately like the highlighted English sounds.

c	q	x	z	zh
pa**ts**	**ch**in	**sh**in	pa**ds**	fu**dge**

2   The six basic vowel sounds are:

a	e	i	o	u	ü
art	h**er**	s**ee**	**o**re	r**u**de	French t**u**

- **i** after **c**, **ch**, **s**, **sh**, **z**, **zh** or **r** loses its basic sound and is almost swallowed up by the preceding consonant.
- **ü** after **j**, **q**, **x** and **y** is written **u** but still pronounced **ü**.
- generally, combined vowels retain their individual basic sound:

ai	**ai**sle	**eng**	hung**er**
iau	m**iaou**	**uo**	**wo**re

But a few sound slightly different:

ang	m**on**ster	**ei**	**eigh**t	**en**	**en**d
iang	**young**	**ui**	**way**		

3   The distinctive sing-song quality of Chinese is due to its tones, of which Mandarin Chinese has four. Each different tone, indicated by a tone mark over the vowel, brings an entirely different meaning to the same combinations of letters: **yū** *silt*, **yú** *fish*, **yǔ** *rain*, **yù** *jade*

1st tone	–	high pitch, flat and steady
2nd tone	´	rising, rather like the query *Yes?*
3rd tone	ˇ	falling then rising, like **Běi** in **Běijīng**
4th tone	`	falling sharply, like **shì** in **shìchǎng**

- A syllable without a tone is pronounced without emphasis.
- An apostrophe is used to separate syllables if there's potential confusion.
- When two third tones or two fourth tones follow each other, the first is said as a second tone: **nǐ** and **hǎo** together sound like **ní hǎo**; **bù** and **shì** together sound like **bú shì**.

Nǐ hǎo

saying hello

... and goodbye

introducing yourself

... and getting to know people

Zài Zhōngguó *In China ...*

the family name, usually a single syllable such as **Wú**, **Lǐ** or **Chén**, comes before the given name. Ms **Wáng**, whose given name is **Wěiléi**, would introduce herself as **Wáng Wěiléi** (although when speaking English she might follow the English order).

The given name on its own is used among family and friends and on less formal occasions, while the full name is used more routinely than in the West. To say hello to Ms **Wáng** you'd say **Wáng Wěiléi, nǐ hǎo**. It's also common for people who know each other to use **xiǎo** *little/young* or **lǎo** *old* with the surname: someone older than **Wáng Wěiléi** could call her **Xiǎo Wáng**, whereas someone younger might use **Lǎo Wáng**.

Saying hello

1   **1•2** Listen to the key language:

hǎo	good/well
Nǐ hǎo.	Hello.
Nín hǎo.	Hello. (more formal)
Nǐ/nín hǎo ma?	How are you?
(Wǒ) hěn hǎo	(I'm) very well
... xièxie. Nǐ ne?	... thank you. You?
Mǎmǎhūhū.	So-so. *Lit*. horse horse tiger tiger

Nǐ hǎo

2   **1•3** Luó Píng, a receptionist at the Zhōngshān Hotel, is arriving at work. Listen and decide how she is – is she well or just so-so?

Zài Zhōngwén lǐ In Chinese ...

when you're addressing more than one person, **nǐ** *you* becomes **nǐmen**.

men can also be added to: **wǒ** *I* – **wǒmen** *we*

tā *he/she/it* – **tāmen** *they*

G3

3   **1•4** Now listen as Luó Píng greets various guests and colleagues at the hotel.

- Does she greet one person or a couple first?
- How many times do you hear **xièxie** *thank you*?

4   **1•5 Hǎo** is also part of **zǎoshang hǎo** *good morning* and **wǎnshang hǎo** *good evening*. During the day, Luó Píng greets the following people. Listen and tick which greeting she uses.

	nǐ hǎo	zǎoshang hǎo	wǎnshang hǎo
Fàn Yǒng			
Wú Lán			
Lǐ xiānsheng *Mr Li*			
Wáng Yáunyuan			
Chén Jiàntāo			

... and goodbye

5   1•6 Listen to the key language:

Zàijiàn

Zàijiàn.	Goodbye. *Lit*. Again see.
Huítóu jiàn.	See you later.
Wǎnshang jiàn.	See you this evening.
Míngtiān jiàn.	See you tomorrow.
Wǎn'ān.	Goodnight. *Lit*. Evening peace.

6   1•7 Listen to Fàn Yǒng saying goodbye to the following people at the Zhōngshān Hotel, and match them with the above phrases.

Lǐ xiānsheng   **Zhào Mǐn**   **Chén tàitai** *Mrs Chén*
Lǐ Yǒng   **Zhào Wěiléi**

7   1•8 Students Tíngting, Léilei and Han leave the lobby next. Listen and jot down in pinyin and English when Han expects to see the others next.

Shénme shíhòu? *When?*
Tíngting ....   **Léilei** ....

8   1•9 You might find it helpful at this point to read about tones on page 6. Then listen to the five ways of saying **ma**, which have entirely different meanings:

mā *mother*   **má** *linen*   **mǎ** *horse*   **mà** *swear*   **ma** *question word*

Now listen and decide which words you hear from these sets.

bái *white*		**bǎi** *hundred*	
é *goose*		**è** *hungry*	
sī *silk*		**sì** *four*	
wō *nest*		**wǒ** *I*	
wū *house*		**wǔ** *five*	
yú *fish*		**yù** *jade*	

Finally, listen and put the correct tone accent on these words.

cha *tea*   **che** *car*   **bei** *north*   **xi** *west*   **wo** *lie*   **lu** *road*   **yu** *rain*

Introducing yourself

1   1•10 Listen to the key language:

Duìbuqǐ.	Excuse me.
Wǒ shì ...	I'm ...
Wǒ bú shì ...	I'm not ...
Nǐ shì ... ma?	Are you ...?
Nín shì Chén xiānsheng ma?	Are you Mr Chén?
shì, shìde/bú shì	yes/no

2   1•11 Luó Píng has a message for a Mr Chén. Listen as she tries to find him in the busy hotel lobby, and tick off the key phrases you hear listed above.

Zài Zhōngwén lǐ In Chinese ...

to make a statement into a question, you just add **ma**:

Tā shì Chén xiānsheng.	He's Mr Chén.
Tā shì Chén xiānsheng ma?	Is he Mr Chén?

---

3   1•12 Listen to someone else checking in at the Zhōngshān Hotel, focus on his name, and decide which of these names is his.

a **Gāo Zhìqiáng**   b **Gāo Zǐxiáng**   c **Gāo Zìxiáng**

Zài Zhōngguó In China ...

a man can be addressed as **xiānsheng**, a woman as **nǚshì** and a younger woman as **xiǎojie**. Or, if you know a woman's married, you can address her as **tàitai**. These words are also used as titles after the name: **Gāo Míng xiānsheng** Mr Gāo Míng; **Huáng Mèngjié nǚshì** Ms Huáng Mèngjié. You never use a title when giving your own name.

---

4   How would you

a   ask a young woman if she's Miss Zhōng,
b   reply if someone asked you that question,
c   say who you are?

... and getting to know people

5 1•14 Listen to the key language:

Nǐ xìng shénme?	What's your surname?
Wǒ xìng ...	My surname is ...
Nǐ jiào shénme?	What's your name?
Wǒ jiào ...	My (full) name's ...
Hěn gāoxìng rènshi nǐ.	Very pleased to meet you.

6 1•15 Listen to Zhào Zhōuzhou saying what her name is when she meets a new colleague. Does she use **Wǒ xìng** or **Wǒ jiào?**

7 1•16 Zhào Zhōuzhōu works on the front desk of a large recruitment company. Listen as she welcomes somebody, and pick out the visitor's names from the following. You might like to refer to page 6 first.

Surname	**Wáng**	**Huáng**	**Hóng**
Given name	**Xuě**	**Qiáng**	**Shēng**

Zài Zhōngwén lǐ In Chinese ...

question words such as *who? what? where?* go in the same position as the answer.

Tā jiào <u>shénme</u>? *What's his/her name? Lit. He/She called what?*

Tā jiào <u>Lǐ Xiǎoyuè</u>. *Her name's Li Xiǎoyuè.* G10

---

8 1•17 Lǐ Xiǎoyuè has arranged to meet someone at the recruitment office. He's older and of a higher social status, so she uses **nín** to convey respect. Listen and complete the conversation, including the tone accents.

- ⚫ .... hǎo. .... shì Wáng Hǎiqìng xiānsheng ....?
- ◆ **Shì,** .... **shì.**
- ⚫ **Wǒ** .... **Lǐ Xiǎoyuè.** .... **gāoxìng rènshi** ....

put it all together

1 Match the Chinese with the English. There's one phrase left over – what does it mean?

a	What's your name?	1	**Hěn gāoxìng rènshi nǐ.**
b	Hello.	2	**Wó hěn hǎo, xièxie.**
c	My name is ...	3	**Nǐ jiào shénme?**
d	Excuse me.	4	**Nǐ hǎo ma?**
e	Good evening.	5	**Duìbuqǐ.**
f	No, I'm not.	6	**Wǎnshang hǎo.**
g	Goodnight.	7	**Nǐ hǎo.**
h	I'm very well, thank you.	8	**Wǒ jiào ...**
i	Very pleased to meet you.	9	**Wǎn'ān.**
		10	**Wǒ bú shì.**

2 What could these people be saying to each other?

1

2

3

4

3 1•18 Here are some Chinese names and words you may find familiar. Try saying them out loud, concentrating on the tones, then listen to the audio to check your pronunciation.

Běijīng	Shànghǎi	Sìchuān	Xī'ān
Máo Zédōng	Hú Jǐntāo		Dèng Xiǎopíng
fēngshuǐ	gōngfu	tàijí	májiàng

now you're talking!

Nǐ hǎo ma?   **Mǎmǎhūhū.**

1 **1•19** Answer as if you were Jake Newman, on holiday in Guangzhou and waiting to go on a tour one morning.

- Say hello to the tour rep.
- ◆ **Zǎoshang hǎo. Nǐ xìng shénme?**
- Give her the information she wants.
- ◆ **Shì Jake Newman xiānsheng ma?**
- Say yes, you're Jake Newman.

- You think you see a famous Chinese actress. Ask the rep if that's **Gǒng Lì**.
- ◆ **Shìde, tā shì Gǒng Lì.**

2 **1•20** On the coach, the person sitting next to you starts a conversation.

- **Zǎoshang hǎo. Wǒ shì Huáng Nà. Nǐ jiào shénme?**
- ◆ Answer her question.
- **Hěn gāoxìng rènshi nǐ.**
- ◆ Say you're pleased to meet her.

When the tour's over you both return to your hotels, having signed up for another tour the next day.

- Say goodbye to Huáng Nà.
- ◆ **Míngtiān jiàn.**

3 **1•21** That evening, you meet a friend, Gāo Wénpíng, in the bar.

- Greet him.
- ◆ **Wǎnshang hǎo.**
- Ask him how he is.
- ◆ **Mǎmǎhūhū. Nǐ ne?**
- Say you're very well, thanks.

quiz

1 When would you use **nǐmen hǎo** instead of **nǐ hǎo?**

2 How might you reply to **nǐ hǎo ma?**

3 What's the difference between **wǎnshang hǎo** and **wǎnshang jiàn?** Can you work out what **míngtiān wǎnshang** means?

4 If someone asks **Tā jiào shénme?**, what do they want to know?

5 When do you say **Hěn gāoxìng rènshi nǐ?**

6 What are the words for *yes* and *no* in reply to *Are you ...?*

7 Who would you address as **tàitai?**

8 Given that *(on) Saturday* is **xīngqīliù**, how do you say *See you on Saturday?*

Now check whether you can ...

- say hello to one person or several people
- say good morning and good evening
- address someone as Mr/Ms/Mrs ...
- ask someone how they are
- reply when someone asks you how you are
- introduce yourself
- reply when someone's introduced to you
- ask someone's name and give your name
- say goodbye

The best way of developing good Chinese pronunciation is by listening to the audio as often as you can and repeating things – out loud – over and over, imitating the speakers closely. It really does make a difference since it familiarises you with the sounds of Chinese and gets you used to the tones, which most people find daunting when they first start learning.

Nǐ shì nǎ guó rén?

talking about nationality

... and where you come from

saying what you do for a living

giving your phone number

Zài Zhōngguó ...

people are delighted to hear visitors speaking their language, and it's worth learning to say a little about yourself and to ask and answer simple questions so that you can make conversation with the people you meet.

When talking about where people are from, the key words are **guó** *country* and **rén** *person*. When you ask what nationality someone is – **Nǐ shì nǎ guó rén?** – literally you're asking *You are which country person?* **Rén** is tacked on to the country for the reply: **Yīngguó** *UK*, **Yīngguórén** *British*; **Měiguó** *USA*, **Měiguórén** *American*. It's not only used with countries: **Běijīngrén** *from Beijing*; **Xiānggǎngrén** *from Hong Kong*.

Talking about nationality

1 1•22 Listen to the key language:

Nǐ shì nǎ guó rén?	What nationality are you?
Wǒ shì Měiguórén.	I'm American.
Nǐ shì Yīngguórén ma?	Are you British?
Shì(de), wǒ shì Yīngguórén.	Yes, I'm British.
Bù, wǒ bú shì Yīngguórén.	No, I'm not British.

2 1•23 Wang Lan, doing some market research for a holiday company, talks to a group of tourists in Beijing. Listen and tick their nationality.

	Yīngguórén	Měiguórén	Xīnxīlánrén *from New Zealand*	Jiānádàrén *Canadian*
Tourist 1				
Tourist 2				
Tourist 3				
Tourist 4				
Tourist 5				

3 1•24 Match these **guójí** *nationalities* to the **guójiā** *countries*. Try saying them out loud, then listen, focusing on the pronunciation.

Wēi'ěrshìrén	Àodàlìyàrén	Sūgélánrén	Yīnggélánrén
Rìběnrén	Ài'ěrlánrén	Hánguórén	Zhōngguórén

guójiā		guójí
Zhōngguó	*China*	....
Hánguó	*Korea*	....
Rìběn	*Japan*	....
Yīnggélán	*England*	....
Sūgélán	*Scotland*	....
Wēi'ěrshì	*Wales*	....
Ài'ěrlán	*Ireland*	....
Àodàlìyà	*Australia*	....

4 How would *you* reply if someone asked **Nǐ shì Yīnggélánrén ma?**

... and where you come from

5 1•25 Listen to the key language:

Nǐ cóng nǎr lái? where come?	Where are you from? *Lit*. You from
Wǒ cóng ... lái.	I come from ... *Lit*. I from ... come.
Nǐ shì běndìrén ma? You are local?	Are you from round here? *Lit*.
Wǒ shì Shànghǎirén.	I'm from Shanghai.
Nǐ yě shì Shànghǎirén ma?	Are you <u>also</u> from Shanghai?
Shì, wó yě shì Shànghǎirén.	Yes, I'm also from Shanghai.

6 1•26 An international group of **xuésheng** *students* are asked by tutors Zhang Li and Zhou Li where they're from. Read the replies, guessing new words or checking them in the glossary, then listen and number them in the order you hear them.

- **Shìde, wǒ shì Shànghǎirén.**
- **Wǒ cóng Měiguó lái, cóng Niǔyuē lái.**
- **Bú shì, wǒ cóng Lúndūn lái.**
- **Wǒ shì Àodàliyàrén, wǒ cóng Xīní lái.**
- **Wǒ cóng Ài'ěrlán lái.**
- **Bù. Wǒ shì Nánjīngrén ... wǒ cóng Nánjīng lái.**

Zài Zhōngwén lǐ ...

like all verbs, **shì** *to be* stays the same regardless of who's talking or being talked about:

> **wǒ shì** *I am*, **wǒmen shì** *we are*

> **nǐ shì**, **nǐmen shì** *you are*

> **tā shì** *he/she/it is*, **tāmen shì** *they are*

Adding **bù** makes it negative:

> **nǐ bú shì** *you're not*, **tāmen bú shì** *they're not*.

In reply to a question containing **shì**, *no* is **bú shì**; *yes* is **shì**, or **shìde** which is slightly more emphatic: *Yes, I am*. **G9**

---

7 1•27 The following place names are written as they're pronounced in Chinese. Work out what they are, then listen as Hannah, Susie and Mark say where they come from and tick the right answer.

Hannah	▢ **Lánkǎisītè**	▢ **Lúndūn**
Susie and Mark	▢ **Jiālǐfúníyà**	▢ **Kānpéilā**

Saying what you do for a living

1 **1•28** Listen to the key language:

Nǐ zuò shénme gōngzuò?	What do you do? *Lit*. You do what work?
Wǒ shì yīshēng/xuésheng.	I'm a doctor/student.
Nǐ yě shì xuésheng ma?	Are you a student too?
Wǒ xué Yīngwén.	I study English.
Wǒ zài yīyuàn gōngzuò.	I work in a hospital. *Lit*. I in hospital work.

2 **1•29** Listen to the people being interviewed about what they do, and number each person's occupation below as you hear it mentioned.

 ....
kuàijìshī

 ....
yīshēng

 ....
dǎoyóu

 ....
lǎoshī

 ....
gōngchéngshī

 ....
fúwùyuán

 ....
lǜshī

 ....
jìzhě

Zài Zhōngwén lǐ ...

word order is very similar to English: subject + verb + object:
Wǒ jiāo Yīngwén. *I teach English.*
However, phrases referring to place or time go before the verb:
Wǒ zài dàxué jiāo Yīngwén. *I teach English at the university.*
Wǒ xīngqīwǔ jiāo Yīngwén. *I teach English on Friday.* **G1**

---

3 **1•30** At a conference, Zhao Li is briefing a visitor. Listen several times and figure out what people do and where they work.

Bāo Yúntiān ....
Liú Chàng ....
Cài Xuán ....
Lín Jiājia ....

dàxúe	*university*
yīyuàn	*hospital*
yínháng	*bank*
gōngchǎng	*factory*
gōngsī	*company*
bàngōngshì	*office*

Giving your phone number

1 **1•31** Listen to the numbers 0 to 10 and practise saying them aloud.

零	一	二	三	四	五	六	七	八	九	十
líng	yī	èr	sān	sì	wǔ	liù	qī	bā	jiǔ	shí
0	1	2	3	4	5	6	7	8	9	10

Zài Zhōngguó …

Arabic numbers are widely used in everyday life. People believe
that 8 is very lucky and 4 is unlucky. Many go to great lengths
to have a phone number or car registration with 8s, and to avoid
one with 4s.

2 **1•32** Listen and jot down the numbers you hear.

……… …… ……… ……… ……… ……… ……… ……… ……… ……

3 **1•33** Now listen to these phrases relating to **diànhuà hàomǎ** *phone
number*.

Nǐde diànhuà hàomǎ shì shénme? What's <u>your</u> phone number?
Wǒde shǒujī hàomǎ shì… <u>My</u> mobile number is …
Gōngsī de diànhuà hàomǎ shì … The <u>company's</u> phone
number is …

4 **1•34** Cài Xuán asks a colleague for her phone number. Try saying her
mobile number before you listen, then make a note of her home **jiā**
and work numbers. In lists of numbers, 1 is pronounced **yāo**, not **yī**, to
avoid confusion with **qī** 7.

Wǒde shǒujī hàomǎ shì 07726 088 098
Wǒ jiā de diànhuà hàomǎ shì …………………
Wǒ gōngsī de diànhuà hàomǎ shì …………………

Zài Zhōngwén lǐ …

de shows possession. It equates to *'s* or *of* in English: **Xuán de** *Xuán's*,
gōngsī de *the company's*. It is also used with **wǒ, nǐ, tā** etc.: **wǒde**
my, **nǐde** *your*, **tāmende** *their*. De is often omitted when referring to
close personal connections: **wǒ māma** *my mother*, **wǒ jiā** *my home*,
nǐ lǎoshī *your teacher*, **tā tóngshì** *his/her colleague*.

G4

put it all together

1 Which answer best fits the question?

a	Nǐ shì Yīnggélánrén ma?	1	Bú shì, wǒ shì jìzhě.
b	Nǐ shì Měiguórén ma?	2	Wǒ shì gōngchéngshī.
c	Nǐde diànhuà hàomǎ shì shénme?	3	Wǒ cóng Sūgélán lái.
d	Nǐ zuò shénme gōngzuò?	4	Bù, wǒ shì Sūgélánrén.
e	Nǐ yě shì lǎoshī ma?	5	Shì qī bā sān wǔ bā jiǔ.
f	Nǐ cóng nǎr lái?	6	Shì, wǒ shì Měiguórén.

2 Yú Jiànzhōng is a doctor from Beijing, and his clinic's telephone number is **líng yāo líng bā wǔ wǔ líng jiǔ yāo liù liù**. How would he complete this form in pinyin? **Zhíyè** is *occupation*.

xìng .... guójí ....

zhíyè .... diànhuà hàomǎ ....

3 Complete this description of Liáng Hǎijiāo from Guǎngzhōu with appropriate words from the box. She's a lawyer, working for a bank.

> cóng   yínháng   lǜshī
> jiào   xìng   lái

Wǒ .... Liáng. Wǒ .... Liáng Hǎijiāo.
Wǒ shì Guǎngzhōurén, wǒ ....
Guǎngzhōu .... Wǒ zài ....
gōngzuò, wǒ shì ....

4 Using 3 as a guide, write down how these people might describe themselves.

Huáng Méilíng
Accountant, works in office
Chinese, from Hong Kong

Rhodri Daniels
Teacher in university
Welsh, from Bangor

now you're talking!

1 **1•35** Take the part of Hannah Pearson in a conversation by answering the questions below, using the information from the business card.

- **Pí'ěrsūn xiǎojie, nǐ shì Měiguórén ma?**
- **Nǐ cóng nǎr lái?**
- **Nǐ zuò shénme gōngzuò?**

> **Name** Hannah Pearson
>
> **Occupation** Lawyer
> **Nationality** British
> **Home Town** Chester

2 **1•36** When on holiday in Xi'an, someone asks you where the university is – and it leads to a conversation.

- **Duìbuqǐ, dàxué zài nǎr?**
- ◆ Tell her you're not from the area.
- **Nǐ shì Jiānádàrén ma? Yīngguórén? Měiguórén?**
- ◆ Say you're British, and find out where she's from.
- **Wǒ shì Yìdàlìrén.**
- ◆ She's Italian. Ask if she's a student.
- **Bù, wǒ jiāo Yìdàlìwén. Nǐ ne?**
- ◆ Tell her you're a teacher too.
- **Wǒ jiào Elena Chéng. Nǐ ne?**
- ◆ Tell her your own name. Now say you're pleased to meet her.
- **Wó yě hěn gāoxìng rènshi nǐ.**

quiz

1 If someone tells you he's **Xiānggǎngrén**, where's he from?

2 Provide the numbers missing from this sequence: **sì ... bā ...**

3 Would **sān bā wǔ jiǔ bā** or **sān sì wǔ èr sì** be the more popular phone number in China?

4 What information do you give if you're asked **nǐde diànhuà hàomǎ shì shénme?**

5 What do you add to **Wáng xiānsheng** to mean *Mr Wáng's*?

6 On a form, what does **zhíyè** mean?

7 Can you find three pairs from the following: **gōngchéngshī, dǎoyóu, xuésheng, yīshēng, dàxué, gōngchǎng, yīyuàn.** What does the remaining word mean?

8 If **Fǎguó** is *France* and **Déguó** is *Germany*, what's the Chinese for French and German nationalities?

Now check whether you can ...

- say what nationality you are
- say where you come from
- say what you do for a living
- ask others for the above information
- use the numbers 0–10
- give your phone number

> Take every opportunity to practise your Chinese: say out loud every number you see; say your **diànhuà hàomǎ** and also the numbers of friends and family; practise introducing yourself and giving your **gōngzuò** and **guójí**. To help you remember new words you could try listing them in a book, putting them on sticky labels in places where you can't fail to notice them or even recording them and comparing your pronunciation with the audio.

Zhè shì wǒ péngyou

introducing friends and colleagues

... and family

saying how old you are

talking about your family

Zài Zhōngguó ...

people are very specific when talking about family relationships.
For example, there are different words for grandparents depending on
whose side of the family they're on: **yéye** and **nǎinai** *paternal grandfather/
grandmother*, **wàigōng** and **wàipó** *maternal grandfather/grandmother*.
And when talking about siblings, the words themselves indicate position in
the family: a brother is **gēge** if he's older and **dìdi** if he's younger; a sister
is **jiějie** if she's older and **mèimei** if she's younger. These words are often
used instead of the given name.

Professional status is reflected in how you address people, with titles such
as **jīnglǐ** *manager*, **zhǔrèn** *director*, **zhǔxí** *chairman*, and **lǎoshī** *teacher* used
routinely after the surname or full name.

Introducing friends and colleagues

1 **1•37** Listen to the key language:

Zhè shì wǒ(de)	This is my
... **péngyou.**	... friend.
... **nǚ péngyou.**	... girlfriend.
... **nán péngyou.**	... boyfriend.
... **tóngshì.**	... colleague.

2 **1•38** David Rees is working in China. Listen as Wáng Lán introduces him to Liáng Xiǎoxiá, and work out

a who Liáng Xiǎoxiá is in relation to Wáng Lán,
b what her professional role is.

Listen again and complete what David says as he hands her his **míngpiàn** *business card*.

● **Wǒ .... David. .... shì .... míngpiàn.**

3 **1•39** Later, Wáng Lán takes David into town to meet various people. You'll hear **Gěi nǐ jièshào** ... *Let me introduce you to* ...

Listen then choose the correct options.

Jiǎng Yuányuan shì Wáng Lán de
- ▪ **tóngshì**
- ▪ **nǚ péngyou**
- ▪ **mèimei**

Huáng Jiànhuán hé Xǔ Qīng shì Wáng Lán de
- ▪ **tóngshì**
- ▪ **péngyou**

What does David say when introduced to Huáng Jiànhuán and Xǔ Qīng?

Zài Zhōngwén lǐ ...

nouns don't add -s or change in any other way in the plural.
Péngyou can mean *friend* or *friends* – it's up to the context to make it clear which it is.

G2

.... and family

4 **1•40** Listen to the key language:

Nà shì wǒ(de)	That is my
... **jiā.**	... family/home.
... **zhàngfu/àiren.**	... husband.
... **tàitai/àiren.**	... wife.
... **érzi.**	... son.
... **nǚ'ér.**	... daughter.
... **bàba hé māma.**	... mother and father.

Zài Zhōngguó ...

àiren, meaning *loved one*, is rather like *spouse* in English, and is widely used instead of the words for husband and wife.

Gěi nǐ jièshào

5 **1•41** Later, David Rees meets up with his sister Jessica, a student. At her hotel they meet Xǔ Qīng and her husband. After listening to the introductions, choose the right options.

Jessica is	☐ younger	☐ older than David
Xǔ Qīng's husband is	☐ Lǎo Dèng	☐ Lǎo Zhèng
They're from	☐ Xiānggǎng	☐ Guǎngzhōu

6 **1•42** Xǔ Qīng shows Jessica and David **tāmen jiā de zhàopiàn** *their family photo*. Remind yourself of the words on page 23, listen, then jot down in Pinyin and English which members of the family are in the photo.

Saying how old you are

1   1•43 Numbers over 10 follow a very logical pattern. Listen to some of these:

11	**shíyī**	21	**èrshíyī**	40	**sìshí**
12	**shí'èr**	22	**èrshí'èr**	50	**wǔshí**
13	**shísān**	23	**èrshísān**	60	**liùshí**
14	**shísì**	24	**èrshísì**	70	**qīshí**
15	**shíwǔ**	25	**èrshíwǔ**	80	**bāshí**
16	**shíliù**	26	**èrshíliù**	90	**jiǔshí**
17	**shíqī**	27	**èrshíqī**	100	**yī bǎi**
18	**shíbā**	28	**èrshíbā**		31 to 99 follow the same pattern
19	**shíjiǔ**	29	**èrshíjiǔ**		as 21 to 29: **sānshíyī, sānshí'èr,**
20	**èrshí**	30	**sānshí**		**sānshísān,** etc.

2   1•44 You're going to hear all but one of the following numbers. Which one is it?

4   5   10   14   40   69   80   96

3   1•45 Say the following numbers out loud:

13   15   39   48   18   24

Then listen to them to see how you did.

4   1•46 Listen to the key language:

Nǐ jǐ suì le?	How old are you? (to young children)
Nǐ duō dà le?	How old are you? (to teenagers or adults)
Nǐ duō dà suìshu le?	How old are you? (to elderly people)
Wǒ/Tā 17 suì.	I am/She is/He is 17.

5   1•47 In China it's quite usual to ask personal questions when you first meet someone. Listen to various members of an extended family being asked how old they are, and make a note of their ages.

....

Talking about your family

6   1•48 Listen to the key language:

Nǐ jiéhūn le ma?	Are you married?
Wǒ jiéhūn le.	I'm married.
Wǒ líhūn le.	I'm divorced.
Wǒ dānshēn.	I'm single.
Nǐ yǒu háizi ma?	Do you have children?
Wǒ yǒu <u>yī</u> ge érzi	I have <u>a</u>/<u>one</u> son
... hé liǎng ge nǚ'ér.	... and two daughters.
Wǒ méi yǒu háizi.	I don't have children.

Zài Zhōngwén lǐ ...

you don't put a noun straight after a number, e.g. one child, two cars. There has to be a measure word (MW) between them, chosen according to what you're talking about. With people, the MW is **ge**: **yī ge péngyou** *one friend*, **sān ge lǎoshī** *three teachers*.

When you're talking about two of something, **liǎng** is used instead of **èr**: **liǎng ge péngyou** *two friends*, **liǎng ge lǎoshī** *two teachers*.

G8

7   1•49 Iwan Jones, in China on a tour, is practising his Chinese on two people he's met, Xiè Zhèngkǎi and Zhōng Jiéníng. Listen to their conversation, and work out whether they're married or not.

8   1•49 Now listen again, this time noting what they say about their families.

	érzi	nǚ'ér
Zhōng Jiéníng		
Xiè Zhèngkǎi		
Iwan Jones		

put it all together

1   Choose the right meaning from the list in the box.

   a **yī ge érzi**
   b **liǎng ge mèimei**
   c **liǎng ge nǚ'ér**
   d **shí'èr ge péngyou**
   e **yī ge gēge**
   f **liǎng ge jiějie**

> **1 older brother, 1 younger brother, 1 son, 2 younger sisters, 2 older sisters, 2 daughters, 2 sons, 2 older brothers, 10 friends, 11 friends, 12 friends**

2   Say the following numbers in Chinese then add the pairs up and say the answers too.

   14 + 36   21 + 22   45 + 54
   12 + 68   81 + 19   77 + 11

3   This is Xiǎoqīng's family tree.

   Choose the correct option.

   a **Jiànzhōng hé Hǎijiāo** ☐ **méi yǒu háizi** ☐ **yǒu sì ge háizi**
   b **Xiǎoqīng yǒu** ☐ **liǎng ge jiějie** ☐ **yī ge jiějie**
   c **Xiǎoqīng de dìdi** ☐ **jiéhūn le** ☐ **dānshēn**
   d **Xiǎoqīng yǒu yī ge** ☐ **nǚ'ér** ☐ **érzi**
   e **Zìqiáng de àiren jiào** ☐ **Tíngting** ☐ **Xiǎoqīng**

now you're talking!

1   **1•50** You're chatting to someone in your hotel and she shows you some photos she's just taken.

- Point to a picture and ask if that's her husband.
- ✦ **Shìde, nà shì wǒde zhàngfu.**
- Now ask if this is her daughter.
- ✦ **Shìde, zhè shì wǒ nǚ'ér.**
- She seems about ten or so. Ask how old she is.
- ✦ **Tā shíyī suì.**
- Tell your English-speaking companion how old the daughter is.

2   **1•51** Read these questions, and answer them when prompted as if you were Steve, married to Olga, with two children Jack (8) and Maya (6). They're from Exeter in the UK.

- **Nǐ hǎo. Nǐ jiào shénme?**
- **Nǐ cóng nǎr lái?**
- **Nǐ jiéhūn le ma?**
- **Nǐ tàitai jiào shénme?**
- **Nǐmen yǒu háizi ma?**
- **Nǐ érzi jǐ suì le?**
- **Nǐ nǚ'ér ne?**

quiz

1 Who is a **dìdi**?

2 If you're told **Zhěngyíng sìshísì suì**, is Zhengying 14, 40 or 44?

3 What's the sum in Chinese of **shí'èr** and **liùshíqī**?

4 What word has to go between **sān** and **péngyou** to say *three friends*?

5 To say you have two children, what goes in the gaps? **Wǒ yǒu .... ge ....**

6 Would you say **nǐ jǐ suì le** or **nǐ duō dà le**? to ask someone in their twenties how old they are?

7 Starting with the youngest, arrange these in order of age: **wǒ wàipó, wǒ nǚ'ér, wǒ tàitai, wǒ māma.**

8 How would you introduce Zhōng Wěi, a company director?

Now check whether you can ...

- introduce friends or colleagues
- say whether you're married or not
- say if you have children
- introduce a member of your family
- use the numbers between 11 to 100
- give your age
- ask how old people of various generations are

A good way to practise talking about your family is to find a **zhàopiàn** *photograph* with lots of them on it – a wedding group is ideal. Point to each person and say their name, who they are in relation to you and how old they are. You might be able to say what some of them do for a living; and if there are different nationalities involved, you could mention that too.

Wǒ yào yī bēi lǜ chá

ordering tea and coffee

... and other drinks

offering someone a drink

making choices

Zài Zhōngguó ...

chá *tea* is a central element of the culture. Whether it's **lǜ chá** *green tea*, **hóng chá** *black (Lit. red) tea*, **wūlóng chá** *oolong tea*, **huā chá** *jasmine tea*, **júhuā chá** *chrysanthemum tea*, or one of the many other varieties available, tea is a symbol of hospitality and respect, drunk on formal and informal occasions. It's believed that each kind of tea has distinctive health-enhancing properties, with green tea being the most beneficial. **Chá** is normally served hot, without milk or sugar, although **nǎi chá** *tea with milk* and **bīng hóng chá** *iced black tea* are increasing in popularity among the younger generation.

Ordering tea and coffee

1 1•52 Listen to the key language:

Nín yào (hē) shénme?	What would you like (to drink)?
Wǒ yào	I'd like, *Lit.* I want
... yī bēi chá/kāfēi.	... one (cup of) tea/coffee.
... yī bēi lǜ chá.	... one (cup of) green tea.
Gěi nín/nǐmen.	Here you are. *Lit.* Give you
Xièxie. – Bú xiè/Bú kèqi.	Thank you. – You're welcome.

Zài Zhōngwén lǐ ...

if you ask for *a tea* or *one coffee,* you need to include the measure word (MW) **bēi** *cup, bowl* or *glass*: **yī bēi chá** *a/one tea,* **liǎng bēi lǜ chá** *two green teas*, **sān bēi kāfēi** *three coffees*.

2 1•53 Listen to various people ordering drinks in a snack bar then complete the conversation. What does the person saying **wǒmen yào** order?

- .... **bēi chá.**
- ◆ **Wǒ yào sān** .... **kāfēi.**
- **Wǒmen** ...... **liǎng bēi** ....
- ◆ **Gěi nǐmen.**
- **Xièxie.**
- ◆ ....

> **Nímen yào shénme?**

3 1•54 Now listen to Lín Guóqiáng and his girlfriend Zhào Měilì ordering tea. Which do they choose?

	绿茶 **lǜ chá** *green tea*	花茶 **huā chá** *jasmine tea*	红茶 **hóng chá** *black tea*
Lín Guóqiáng			
Zhào Měilì			

... and other drinks

4 **1•55** Listen to the key language:

yī guàn píjiǔ	one can of beer
liǎng guàn píjiǔ	two cans of beer
yī píng pútáojiǔ	one bottle of wine
liǎng píng júzi zhī/kělè	two bottles of orange juice/cola
sān píng (kuàngquán) shuǐ	three bottles of (mineral) water

Zài Zhōngwén lǐ ...

the measure word for something in a can or a tin is **guàn**, and a
bottle **píng**. If ever you forget which measure word to use, you
can get away with using **ge** without the noun: **Wǒ yào sān guàn
píjiǔ** *I'd like three beers* or **Wǒ yào sān ge** *I'd like three (of them)*.

---

5 **1•56** Listen to Wáng Guānxiù ordering beer and cola in a **jiǔbā** *bar* and
note how many of each he wants.

啤酒 可乐
.... **píjiǔ** .... **kělè**

6 **1•57** The **jiǔbā** is busy. Listen as the waiter takes a drinks order for a
party and make a note of what people ask for.

7 How would you order the following?

2 cups of tea
1 glass of water
1 bottle of mineral water
5 cans of cola
6 glasses of beer
1 bottle of wine
4 glasses of orange juice

Offering someone a drink

1   **1•58** Listen to the key language:

Qǐng jìn/zuò.	Please come in/sit down.
Qǐng hē chá.	Please have some tea.
Wǒ hē hóng chá.	I'll have black tea.
Nǐ yào jiā niúnǎi ma?	Would you like it with milk?
Nǐ yào jiā táng ma?	Would you like it with sugar?
Hǎo, xièxie./Bú yào, xièxie.	Yes, please./No, thank you.
Zhè ge chá hěn hǎohē.	This tea is delicious.

2   **1•59** Lǐ Wěi welcomes Zhāng Méi and Jon Riley, an American colleague, to his office. Listen and decide what sort of tea they both have and whether either of them takes milk and sugar.

Zhāng Méi ....   Jon Riley ....

> **Zài Zhōngwén lǐ ...**
>
> there's no direct translation of *please. Yes, please* is **Hǎo, xièxie,** and *please (do something)* is **qǐng** as in **qǐng zuò. Qǐng** literally means *invite* and can be used to offer to buy a drink: **Wǒ qǐng nǐ/nǐmen** *It's my round.* Sometimes, *please* is conveyed with **ba**: **Hē ba** *Please drink.*

3   **1•60** Zhāng Méi visits Lín Guóqiáng the following day. Their conversation is below, but not in the right order. Rearrange the phrases, then listen to see if you got it right.

- **Nǐ hǎo, Zhāng Méi, qǐng jìn.**
- ◆ **Xièxie.**
- **Wǒ hěn hǎo. Qǐng zuò. Nǐ hē chá ma?**
- ◆ **Qǐng hē chá.**
- **Zhè ge chá hěn hǎohē.**
- ◆ **Xièxie, Lín xiānsheng, nín hǎo ma?**
- **Wǒ yào hóng chá.**

Making choices

1 **1•61** Listen to the key language:

Nǐmen yào ...	Would you like ...
... chá háishi kāfēi?	... tea or coffee?
... bái (pútáojiǔ) háishi hóng (pútáojiǔ)?	... white (wine) or red (wine)?
Wǒmen dōu yào chá.	We'd <u>all</u>/<u>both</u> like tea.
Wǒ yě yīyàng.	The same for me.
Gān bēi!	Cheers!

2 **1•62** Jon Riley goes back to see Lǐ Wěi the next day with German colleagues Elke Braun and Eric Hollmann. Listen to the conversation then make a note of what's offered to them and what they accept.

- .... **háishi** ....
- Jon .... Elke .... Eric ....

> **Zài Zhōngwén lǐ ...**
>
> in a question, *or* is **háishi**. When **háishi** appears in a question, **ma** is not needed at the end.
>
> **Nǐ yào chá háishi kāfēi?** *Would you like tea or coffee?*
>
> **Tāmen shì Yīngguórén háishi Měiguórén?** *Are they English or American?*
>
> G10

3 **1•63** After work, Zhāng Méi is meeting Jon and a friend Lisa in a **kāfēiguǎn** *café*. Listen and tick what they have to drink.

	píjiǔ	kuàngquán shuǐ	bái pútáojiǔ	hóng pútáojiǔ	júzi zhī
Zhāng Méi					
Jon					
Lisa					

4 How would you offer someone these choices?

a green tea or jasmine tea?
b red or white wine?
c mineral water or orange juice?
d beer or cola?

put it all together

1 Choose an appropriate response from the box below.

  a **Xièxie**
  b **Nín yào hē shénme?**
  c **Qǐng zuò**
  d **Nǐmen yào chá háishi kāfēi?**
  e **Nǐ yào jiā niúnǎi ma?**

> **Gān bēi**   **Hěn hǎo**   **Xièxie**   **Wǒ yào yī bēi lǜ chá**
> **Bú kèqi**   **Bú yào, xièxie**   **Wǒmen dōu hē chá**

2 What has been ordered to drink here?

  a **sān bēi hóng pútáojiǔ, yī píng kělè**
  b **liǎng bēi hóng chá, wǔ bēi kāfēi, yī bēi bīng hóng chá**
  c **jiǔ guàn júzi zhī, sì píng kuàngquán shuǐ**
  d **yī píng píjiǔ, yī bēi bái pútáojiǔ, liǎng guàn kělè**

3 For each of these, write the number in pinyin and replace the picture with the correct measure word.

  a 1   **hóng pútáojiǔ**   e 4   **kāfēi**
  b 6   **píjiǔ**   f 3   **píjiǔ**
  c 2   **júzi zhī**   g 5   **bái pútáojiǔ**
  d 7   **nǎi chá**   h 1   **kuàngquán shuǐ**

4 Rearrange the words to make sentences.

  a **shénme yào hē nín?**
  b **zhè ge hǎohē hěn chá**
  c **háishi yào nǐmen kuàngquán shuǐ júzi zhī?**
  d **kělè yào píng yī wǒ**

now you're talking!

1 **1•64** You're in a tea shop, about to order for yourself and two friends who don't speak Chinese.

- Nǐmen hǎo. Nǐmen yào shénme?
- ◆ Say you all want tea.
- Nǐmen yào shénme chá? Hóng chá, lǜ chá háishi huā chá?
- ◆ Order a green tea for yourself.
- Tāmen yào shénme chá?
- ◆ Say they want a black tea and a jasmine tea.
- Hǎo de. ... Gěi nǐmen chá.

2 **1•65** You've just arrived at Guómào Trading Company where you have an appointment.

- Nín hǎo. Qǐng jìn, qǐng zuò.
- ◆ Say thank you.
- Bú xiè. Nín hē chá háishi kāfēi ?
- ◆ You'll have tea, please.
- Nín yào lǜ chá háishi hóng chá?
- ◆ Go for the black tea.
- Nín yào jiā niúnǎi ma? Nín yào jiā táng ma?
- ◆ You don't want them.
- Gěi nín.
- ◆ Say the tea's delicious.

3 **1•66** Now, in a **jiǔbā** with a friend, you're going to have the following conversation.

- Ask your friend if he'd like some beer. You're buying.
- ◆ He says he'd like red wine.
- Order a glass of red wine for him and a bottle of beer for yourself.
- ◆ When the drinks arrive, say *Cheers!*

quiz

1 When accepting the offer of a drink, how do you say *please* in Chinese?

2 How do you respond when someone says **xièxie** to you?

3 To say you'd like some red wine, would you add **bái** or **hóng** to **Wǒ yào .... pútáojiǔ?**

4 If you hear **Qǐng zuò**, what are you being invited to do?

5 Would you use **bēi**, **ge**, **píng** or **guàn** when asking for two bottles of beer?

6 If you're not sure of the correct measure word, which should you go for?

7 To offer someone some tea or coffee, what would you need to add to **Nǐ yào chá .... kāfēi?**

8 If **Bú yào bīng, xièxie** is *No ice, thank you*, how would you say you don't want milk?

Now check whether you can ...

- ask for a coffee or a cup of various types of tea
- order one or more cold drinks in a bar
- offer someone a drink
- accept or say no thank you when you're offered a drink
- pay a compliment on receiving a cup of tea
- respond when someone thanks you

> The way to get used to measure words is to use them every day. When you have a coffee or a beer or a glass of water, say what you're drinking in Chinese and include the measure word after **yī** (or other numbers if you're with someone else).
>
> As your vocabulary increases you'll come across more MWs which you can add to your list of things you regularly say in Chinese. For example, **běn** is used for any kind of book, **bāo** for anything in a packet and **liàng** for things with wheels, e.g. cars, buses, bikes.

Checkpoint 1

1

qǐng jìn

bú kèqi

nǐ hǎo

wǎn'ān

hěn gāoxìng rènshi nǐ

wǒ hěn hǎo, xièxie

zhè shì wǒde míngpiàn

míngtiān jiàn

nǐ duō dà le?

mǎmǎhūhū

wǒ bú yào, xièxie

zǎoshang hǎo

qǐng zuò

zhè shì wǒde wàigōng

zhè ge chá hěn hǎohē

Which expression would you use …
a to greet somebody in the morning
b when you're introduced to someone
c to say your tea's delicious
d to say you're very well
e to invite someone to sit down
f to decline something, for example a drink
g in reply to *thank you*
h to ask how old someone is
i to say goodnight
j when presenting a business card

2 Identify the odd one out.

a	pútáojiǔ	júzi zhī	jiǔbā	píjiǔ	kuàngquán shuǐ
b	èrshíqī	shísān	bǎi	liùshíyī	guó
c	Yīngwén	érzi	zhàngfu	nǚ'ér	mèimei
d	Yīnggélán	Sūgélán	Wēi'ěrshì	Àodàlìyà	Ài'ěrlán
e	bēi	ge	guàn	píng	shuǐ
f	zhǔxí	jīnglǐ	wàipó	tóngshì	zhǔrèn
g	dǎoyóu	péngyou	jìzhě	yīshēng	gōngchéngshī
h	niúnǎi	kāfēi	chá	táng	líng

3 The proprietor of your holiday hotel has asked if you'd help his teenage niece fill in a form for an English course in London. What are the questions you need to ask her before you can fill this in?

> Name: ....
> Age: ....
> Nationality: ....
> Occupation: ....

a ....
b ....
c ....
d ....

4 Are these answers right or wrong? Correct any wrong ones.

a 11 + 14 = **èrshí-liù**   b 40 + 7 = **sānshí-qī**
c 50 + 2 = **wǔshí-èr**   d 60 + 34 = **liùshí-bā**

A good way of practising low numbers is to throw two dice and say aloud the possible number combinations. For example:

3 **sān**
5 **wǔ**
35 **sānshíwǔ**
53 **wǔshísān**

Three dice will let you go further and practise the hundreds.

5 **1•67** Listen to the international dialling codes for these countries and add the missing numbers. Can you guess what the countries are?

Xiānggǎng	00 852	Rìběn	00 ....
Yìndùníxīyà	00	Tàiguó	00 ....
Xīnjiāpō	00	Yuènán	00 ....
Mǎláixīyà	00	Fēilǜbīn	00 ....

Now say your phone number, complete with the international code.

6   **1•68** Practise saying the names of some of China's major cities, paying careful attention to the tones. Then listen to check your pronunciation.

Xī'ān	Luòyáng	Chóngqìng	Chéngdū
Hā'ěrbīn	Sūzhōu	Tiānjīn	Guǎngzhōu
Shēnzhèn	Xīshuāngbǎnnà		

7   **1•69** While waiting at Beijing Airport you overhear two young people getting to know each other. Listen, then complete this profile of Nicola by ticking the right information.

You'll hear a new question:

Nǐ lái Zhōngguó dùjià háishi gōngzuò? *Are you in China on holiday or for work?*

Nicola shì	☐ Yīngguórén	☐ Měiguórén
Nicola de māma shì	☐ Zhōngguórén	☐ Měiguórén
Nicola zài Zhōngguó	☐ dùjià	☐ gōngzuò
Tā	☐ èrshíyī suì	☐ èrshíqī suì
Tā shì	☐ xuésheng	☐ yīshēng
Tāde bàba shì	☐ yīshēng	☐ gōngchéngshī

Guóqiáng invites Nicola for a drink **Wǒ qǐng nǐ hē píjiǔ**. What does she have?

8 Here are the Chinese characters for the numbers 1 to 5:

一	二	三	四	五

Have a look at some more:

10	**shí**	十
11	**shíyī**	十一
20	**èrshí**	二十
25	**èrshíwǔ**	二十五

Can you say what the following are?

a 十三　　　　b 十五　　　　c 二十二　　　d 三十

9 Now find some patterns relating to nationality.

Wǒ shì 我是　　　　**Nǐ shì** 你是　　　**Tā shì** 他是

Nǐ shì nǎ guó rén? 你 是 哪 国 人

Zhōngguó 中国	**Zhōngguórén** 中国人
Yīngguó 英国	**Yīngguórén** 英国人
Měiguó 美国	**Měiguórén** 美国人

Can you work out what these say?

a 我 是 中 国 人

b 他 是 美 国 人

10 Now for some drinks.

lǜ chá 绿茶	**kuàngquán shuǐ** 矿泉水
huā chá 花茶	**bái pútáojiǔ** 白葡萄酒
hóng chá 红茶	**hóng pútáojiǔ** 红葡萄酒

Decide which of these means red, white, tea and water.

a 茶　　　　b 水　　　　c 白　　　　d 红

Yǒu shìchǎng ma?

asking what there is in town

... and whereabouts it is

finding out how far places are

... and when they're open

Zài Zhōngguó ...

the local 旅游局 lǚyóu jú *tourist office* in the main towns are generally administrative bodies, so if you want to find out what to see and do, the hotel reception is your best starting point.

Distances are measured using the metric system, based on the mǐ *metre* and gōnglǐ *kilometre*. You might occasionally still hear lǐ, a traditional Chinese unit of distance now standardised to 500 metres. It features in the traditional name for the Great Wall of China **Wàn Lǐ Chángchéng**, literally *the 10,000 lǐ wall*, a symbolic name intended to convey the immeasurable nature of the Wall but which, in reality, underestimates the actual length.

Asking what there is in town

1   **1•70** Listen to the key language:

Yǒu cānguǎn.	There's a restaurant.
Yǒu hěnduō cānguǎn.	There are many restaurants.
Qǐng wèn ...	Please may I ask ...
Yǒu shìchǎng ma?	Is there a market?
Zhèr yǒu wǎngbā ma?	Is there an internet café <u>here</u>?
Méi yǒu gōngyuán.	There isn't a park.

Zài Zhōngwén lǐ ...

yǒu means *have* and also *there is/there are*. The negative uses **méi**, rather than **bù** like other verbs in the present tense:

yǒu chāojí shìchǎng *there's a supermarket*; **méi yǒu** chāojí shìchǎng <u>*there's no*</u> *supermarket*.

wǒ yǒu yī ge érzi *I have one son*; **wǒ méi yǒu háizi** *I <u>don't have</u> children*.

In reply to a question using **yǒu** or **méi yǒu**, *yes* is **yǒu** and *no* is **méi yǒu**.

---

2   Have a look at this list of places and practise saying them.

shāngdiàn	shìchǎng	chāojí shìchǎng	yínháng	wǎngbā
商店	市场	超级市场	银行	网吧
shop	*market*	*supermarket*	*bank*	*internet café*

cānguǎn	xīcānguǎn	gōngyuán	huāyuán	bówùguǎn
餐馆	西餐馆	公园	花园	博物馆
restaurant	*Western restaurant*	*park*	*gardens*	*museum*

3   **1•71** Tour guide Xin Liu tells a group of visitors some basic facts about her town. Listen and pick out the four places she mentions.

4   **1•72** Now listen as people ask her questions, and tick or cross the availability of the following. **Fúzhuāng** means *clothes*.

internet café   ▢   Western restaurant   ▢
clothes market   ▢   museum   ▢

... and whereabouts it is

5   **1•73** Listen to the key language:

Bówùguǎn   The museum
... zài **shì zhōngxīn**.   ... is in the <u>town centre</u>.
... zài shì zhōngxīn **de běi biān** ... is <u>to the north</u> of the town centre
... zài **yínháng duìmiàn**.   ... is opposite the bank.
... zài **yínháng pángbiān**.   ... is next to the bank.

6   **1•74** Xin Liu is using this map of the town centre to explain where places are. Check you know what the named places are, then listen and work out what A, B and C represent.

běi 北

shì zhōngxīn

C

B huāyuán

A gōngyuán

huǒchēzhàn

Zài Zhōngwén lǐ ...

zài is used to say where something is, translating words like *in*, *at* or *on* according to the context. It also translates *is/are in*, *at* or *on* without the need for the verb **shì** *to be*.

7   **1•75** Listen as Xin Liu is asked again if there's a clothes market. In her reply you'll hear **huǒchēzhàn** *train station*. Is the market next to or opposite the station?

Finding out how far places are

1   1•76 Listen to the key language:

Fùjìn yǒu méi yǒu gōngyuán?	Is there a park <u>nearby</u>?
Gōngyuán lí zhèr <u>yuǎn</u> ma?	Is the park <u>far</u> from here?
Bù yuǎn, hěn jìn.	Not far, very near.
wǔ bǎi <u>mǐ</u>/liǎng <u>gōnglǐ</u> yuǎn	500 <u>metres</u>/2 <u>kilometres</u> away
zǒulù èrshí fēnzhōng	20 minutes' walk *Lit.* walk
20 minutes	

Zài Zhōngwén lǐ ...

Yǒu méi yǒu ...? is a very common alternative to Yǒu ... ma?
for *Is/Are there ...?* or *Have you got ...?*
Běijīng yǒu méi yǒu gōngyuán? *Are there parks in Beijing?*
Nǐ yǒu méi yǒu háizi? *Do you have children?*
The same structure (verb + negative + same verb) works with
other verbs too, e.g. **Shì bú shì ...?** as an alternative to **Shì ...
ma?** for *Are you/is he/she?* etc. This would be the equivalent of
Are you or are you not ...?

2   1•77 Xin Liu's group is exploring without her, and Harry's looking for
a bank. Listen and decide where it is and how long it will take him to
walk there.

3   1•78 Anna's looking for a supermarket. First, remind yourself which of
these words means supermarket:

   ● **shìchǎng**   ● **cānguǎn**   ● **chāojí shìchǎng**   ● **shāngdiàn**

Then listen and work out how far it is.

4   1•79 Anna then asks whether there's a **yóuyǒngchí** *swimming pool*
and is told it's <u>to the west</u> of the town centre: **Yóuyǒngchí zài shì
zhōngxīn <u>de xī biān</u>**. Listen and work out what she's told about
getting there.

... and when they're open

5   1•80 Listen to the key language:

... jīntiān/míngtiān kāimén ma?	Is ... open today/tomorrow?
... xīngqīyī kāimén ma?	Is ... open on Monday?
... měi tiān kāimén.	... is open every day.
... xīngqītiān guānmén.	... is closed on Sunday.

xīngqīyī	星期一	Monday
xīngqī'èr	星期二	Tuesday
xīngqīsān	星期三	Wednesday
xīngqīsì	星期四	Thursday
xīngqīwǔ	星期五	Friday
xīngqīliù	星期六	Saturday
xīngqītiān/xīngqīrì	星期天	Sunday

6   1•81 Xin Liu is telling Harry which days the swimming pool and the **táocí bówùguǎn** *porcelain museum* are open and when there's a **zhǎnlǎnhuì** *exhibition* in town. Listen and fill the gaps. How would Harry relay this information in English?

- **Yóuyǒngchí** .... **kāimén.**
- **Táocí bówùguǎn** ...., ... **hé** .... **guānmén.**
- .... **yǒu zhǎnlǎnhuì.**

> **Zài Zhōngguó ...**
>
> the day is divided into five: **zǎoshang** early morning; **shàngwǔ** about 9am until noon; **zhōngwǔ** noon; **xiàwǔ** afternoon until about 6pm; **wǎnshang** after 6pm. These are used with **jīntiān**, **míngtiān** and the days of the week, e.g. **míngtiān xiàwǔ** *tomorrow afternoon*, **xīngqīwǔ wǎnshang** *Friday evening*.

7   1•82 Listen to Xin Liu giving the opening hours for the **yóujú** *post office*, then number the following times 1 or 2 according to whether it's open or closed at that time.

1 **yóujú** ...... **kāimén**	2 **yóujú** ...... **guānmén**
xīngqīliù xiàwǔ ▢	xīngqīliù wǎnshang ▢
xīngqīliù shàngwǔ ▢	xīngqītiān zǎoshang ▢
xīngqītiān wǎnshang ▢	

put it all together

1   Match the phrases.

a	**Gōngyuán bù yuǎn**	1	There's no supermarket nearby
b	**Méi yǒu wǎngbā**	2	There are lots of shops
c	**Bówùguǎn zài yínháng duìmiàn**	3	The museum is opposite the bank
d	**Fùjìn méi yǒu chāojí shìchǎng**	4	The bank is next to the market
e	**Zǒulù èrshìwǔ fēnzhōng**	5	The park isn't far
f	**Yǒu hěnduō shāngdiàn**	6	Twenty-five minutes' walk
g	**Yínháng zài shìchǎng pángbiān**	7	There's no internet café

2   Have a look at these notices then answer the questions.

Zhōngguó yínháng
Bank of China
xīngqīyī – xīngqīliù:
shàngwǔ 8:00 – xiàwǔ 5:00
xīngqītiān: shàngwǔ 9:00 – xiàwǔ 4:00

Xīnghǎi yīnyuè tīng
Xinghai Concert Hall
xīngqīwǔ – xīngqīliù:
wǎnshang 7:00–10:30

Táoyuán gējùyuàn
Taoyuan Opera House
xīngqīyī – xīngqīwǔ: xiàwǔ 2:00–5:00
wǎnshang 6:30–10:00
xīngqīliù – xīngqītiān: xiàwǔ 2:00–5:00

Mínzú Huàláng
Gallery of Folk Art
xīngqīyī – xīngqīliù:
shàngwǔ 9:00 – xiàwǔ 6:00

   a   Which day is the Gallery of Folk Art closed?
   b   What are the opening hours for the Bank of China?
   c   What time can you see an opera on Friday?
   d   Is there a concert mid-week at the Xinghai Concert Hall?

3   Using **Wǒde chéngshì** (*town*) **yǒu/méi yǒu …** *In my town there is/there isn't …*, say whether your home town has some of the places mentioned in this unit. The measure word you'll need is **jiā**, e.g. **yǒu sān jiā yínháng** *there are 3 banks*.

now you're talking!

1   **1•83** You're in Shenzhen, and you ask a man waiting at a bus stop for some information.

- Say *Excuse me* and ask if there's a park.
- ◆ **Yǒu. Hěn jìn – wǔ bǎi mǐ.**
- Now ask if there are any shops here.
- ◆ **Yǒu hěnduō shāngdiàn; zài shì zhōngxīn.**
- Thank him and say goodbye.
- ◆ **Bú xiè. Zàijiàn.**

2   **1•84** Later, you need to contact home so you stop someone else.

- Say *Excuse me* and ask if there's an internet café nearby.
- ◆ **Méi yǒu. Wǎngbā zài shì zhōngxīn de běi biān. Yuǎn, hěn yuǎn, wǔ gōnglǐ.**
- Pity. Now ask if the post office is far from here.
- ◆ **Yóujú bù yuǎn. Zài shì zhōngxīn , yínháng pángbiān.**
- Repeat the information you've been given and thank him.
- ◆ **Bú kèqi.**
- Now ask if the bank's open today.
- ◆ **Jīntiān yínháng guānmén.**
- Ask if it's open tomorrow.
- ◆ **Shìde. Míngtiān kāimén.**

quiz

1 What do you add to the beginning of a question to make it more polite?

2 Which is the odd one out: **shìchǎng shāngdiàn yóuyǒngchí chāojí shìchǎng**? What does it mean?

3 In China, is 3pm classed as **zhōngwǔ** or **xiàwǔ**?

4 If something is described as **zài chāojí shìchǎng pángbiān**, is it next to or opposite the supermarket?

5 Can you think of another way of asking **Yǒu xīcānguǎn ma?**

6 What's the opposite of these words? **yǒu, kāimén, yuǎn**

7 Would you expect the Bank of China to be open **xīngqīliù shàngwǔ?**

8 What would you need to add to **Yǒu … cānguǎn** to say there are *many* restaurants?

Now check whether you can ...

- approach someone politely
- understand and say the words for places in town
- ask if there's a particular place nearby
- understand basic phrases describing where a place is
- ask if a place is open
- recognise the days of the week
- recognise parts of the day

Practise the language of this unit by imagining you're telling a Chinese visitor when places are open where you live, for example, banks, supermarkets, swimming pool, library **túshūguǎn**. Writing the information down in pinyin, making sure you include the tone marks, will really help you to focus on the sounds – as well as to remember the words.

Shì zhōngxīn zài nǎr?

asking the way

... and following directions

talking about where people live

getting help to understand

Zài Zhōngguó ...

the points of the compass are **dōng** *east*, **nán** *south*, **xī** *west*, **běi** *north*, said in that order. They're regularly used when giving directions, and are a feature of numerous place names such as **Shāndōng**, **Xī'an** and, of course, **Běijīng** and **Nánjīng**, literally *north capital* and *south capital*, dating from when China was divided by the Yangtze river into two kingdoms. Historically, **zhōng** *central* was linked with **dōng**, **nán**, **xī** and **běi**, and **Zhōngguó** *China* literally means *Middle Kingdom*.

Other words that feature regularly in place names include **hǎi** *sea*, **hé** *river*, **hú** *lake*, **shān** *mountain*, **shěng** *province* and **shì** *city*.

Asking the way

1 **2•1** Listen to the key language:

... zài nǎr?	Where is/are ...?
Zuìjìn de ... zài nǎr?	Where is/are the nearest ...?
... zài yī/èr/sān céng floor	... is/are on the ground/first/second
... zài lóushàng/lóuxià	... is/are upstairs/downstairs
... zài nǐde <u>zuǒ</u>/<u>yòu</u> biān	... is/are on your <u>left</u>/<u>right</u>
Jiù zài nàbiān.	It's/they're just over there.
Duìbuqǐ, wǒ bù dǒng/zhīdao.	Sorry, I don't understand/know.

2 **2•2** In a shopping centre, Tom Stratton asks where the toilets are. Listen, tick what he's told, then explain in English where they are.

Cèsuǒ zài ... lóushàng ▩ **lóuxià** ▩ **èr céng** ▩ **sān céng** ▩ **sì céng** ▩

3 **2•3** He doesn't find them so he asks again. You'll hear **Wǒ dǒng le** *I understand now*. Listen and:

a note in Chinese how the first person replies ....
b say where the second person says they are ....

Zài Zhōngguó ...

floors are numbered as in the US, i.e. UK ground floor is **yī céng**, UK first floor is **èr céng** and so on; and they tend to be numbered *one*, *two*, *three*, etc. rather than *first*, *second*, *third*. To avoid the unlucky associations of 13 for westerners and 14 for local people, many high rise blocks no longer have a 13th or a 14th floor. Instead they have **12 céng**, **12 céng A** and **12 céng B**.

---

4 **2•4** Having found the right floor, Tom gets the information he needs. Listen and fill the gaps. Are the toilets on the left or on the right?

● **Qǐng wèn, cèsuǒ ....?**
◆ **Cèsuǒ zài nǐde .... biān. Jiù .... nàbiān.**

 男 **nán**

 女 **nǚ**

... and following directions

5 **2•5** Listen to the key language:

Qù ... zěnme zǒu?	How do I get to ...? *Lit.* ... how go?
Zǒu dào lùkǒu.	Go as far as the crossroads.
Zǒu dào dì yī ge hónglǜdēng.	Go as far as the <u>first</u> traffic lights.
Yìzhí zǒu.	Go straight on.
Wǎng <u>dōng</u>/<u>nán</u>/<u>xī</u>/<u>běi</u> zǒu.	Go <u>east</u>/<u>south</u>/<u>west</u>/<u>north</u>.
Lit. Toward ... go.	
Wǎng <u>zuǒ</u>/<u>yòu</u> guǎi.	Turn <u>left</u>/<u>right</u> *Lit.* Toward ... turn.
Duì.	That's correct.

6 **2•6** Tom's looking for the **huǒchēzhàn** *train station*. Listen and pick out from the above list the three pieces of information he's given.

7 **2•7** He now wants to go to Xuéyuàn Road and asks: **Qù Xuéyuàn Lù zěnme zǒu?** Listen to the reply and tick the correct option.

Wǎng	☐ **dōng**	☐ **nán**	☐ **xī**	☐ **běi zǒu**
Zǒu dào	☐ **lùkǒu**	☐ **hónglǜdēng**		
Wǎng	☐ **dōng**	☐ **xī**	☐ **zuǒ**	☐ **yòu guǎi**
Xuéyuàn Lù zài	☐ **zuǒ**	☐ **yòu biān**		

Zài Zhōngwén lǐ ...

to say *first*, *second*, *third* etc, you simply put **dì** before the number:
dì yī *first*, **dì èr** *second*, **dì wǔ** *fifth*. The normal measure word is
needed before a noun: **dì èr ge hónglǜdēng** *the second traffic lights*.

---

8 **2•8** The directions were wrong. Explaining he's lost: **Wǒ mí lù le**, Tom asks again. Listen and work out whether Xuéyuàn Road is A, B or C on the map.

Talking about where people live

1 2•9 Listen to the key language:

Nǐ zhù zài nǎr?	Where do you live? *Lit.* you live in where?
Wǒ/Wǒmen zhù zài Shànghǎi.	I/We live in Shanghai.
Wǒ dìdi bú zhù zài Shànghǎi.	My brother doesn't live in Shanghai.
Nǐ dìdi zhù zài nǎr?	Where does your brother live?
Tā zhù zài jiāoqū/hǎi biān.	He/She lives in the suburbs/by the sea.
Tāmen zhù zài nóngcūn.	They live in the country.

2 2•10 Féng Yīmín, a Chinese student in the UK, is asking a group of language students where they live. Listen and tick who lives where. Listen out for **yě** *also*.

	town centre	country	suburbs	seaside
George				
Jacquie				
Fran				
Thomas				
Lizzie				

3 2•11 Yīmín then says where she and some other people live. Check that you remember who the following are, then listen and make a note of where they all live. You'll hear **dànshì** *but*.

Féng Yīmín .... **Tā jiějie** ....

Tā bàba hé māma .... **Tā yéye hé nǎinai** ....

Zài Zhōngwén lǐ ...

unlike in many other languages, verbs, e.g. **zhù** *to live*, **gōngzuò** *to work*, **zhīdao** *to know*, **dǒng** *to understand*, **shì** *to be*, stay unchanged regardless of who's talking or being talked about.

To make a sentence negative in the present tense, you put **bù** before the verb: **Wǒ (bù) zhù zài Shànghǎi** *I (don't) live in Shanghai*. The only exception is **yǒu** *to have*, which becomes **méi yǒu**. **G9**

Getting help to understand

4   2•12 Listen to the key language:

Qǐng zài shuō yībiàn.	Please say it again.
Qǐng shuō màn yìdiǎn.	Please speak more slowly.
Nǐ huì shuō Yīngyǔ ma?	Can you speak English?
Bú huì/Huì. Huì shuō yìdiān.	No/Yes. I can speak a little.
Nǐde Yīngyǔ hěn hǎo.	Your English is very good.
Nǎli, nǎli!	Not at all!

5   2•13 Listen as Yīmìn introduces her friend Měilì, who talks about her **gōngyù** *apartment*.

   a   Where is it? .... **b**   Which floor is it on? ....

6   2•14 Měilì continues but George loses the drift. Read their conversation, anticipating how the new words in the box will sound, listen with the text, then listen again with your book closed.

- **Wǒ shēng zài Sūzhōu, xiànzài zhù zài Shànghǎi.**
- ◆ **Qǐng zài shuō yībiàn.**
- **Wǒ zhù zài Shànghǎi, dànshì wǒ shēng zài Sūzhōu.**
- ◆ **Duìbuqǐ Měilì, wǒ bù dǒng. Nǐ huì shuō Yīngyǔ ma?**
- **Huì shuō Yìdiǎn.** I was born in Sūzhōu but now – **xiànzài** – I live in Shànghai.
- ◆ **Nǐde yīngyǔ hěn hǎo!**
- **Nǎli, nǎli.**

> **Wǒ shēng** *I was born*; **xiànzài** *now*

Zài Zhōnggwén lǐ ...

adding **wén** or **yǔ** *language* to the first syllable of many countries gives you the language: **Zhōngguó** *China*, **Zhōngwén** *Chinese*; **Yīngguó** *UK*, **Yingwén/Yīngyǔ** *English*; **Fǎguó** *France*, **Fǎwén/Fǎyǔ** *French*, **Rìběn** *Japan*, **Rìwén/Rìyǔ** *Japanese*.

For some languages, **wén/yǔ** is added to the entire country name: **Xībānyá** *Spain*, **Xībānyáwén/Xībānyáyǔ** *Spanish*. **Yǔ** refers more to spoken language and **wén** to written language.

put it all together

1 Find the corresponding Chinese phrase. Which one is left over? What does it mean?

a	Please say it again	1	Qǐng shuō màn yìdiǎn
b	Do you live in Germany?	2	Nǐ shuō Déwén ma?
c	I don't know	3	Wǒ bù dǒng
d	I speak a little bit of Chinese	4	Wǎng dōng guǎi
e	Please speak more slowly	5	Wǒ bù zhīdao
f	Do you speak German?	6	Nǐ zhù zài Déguó ma?
g	I don't understand	7	Wǒ shuō yìdiǎn Zhōngwén
		8	Qǐng zài shuō yībiàn

2 Fill the gaps with the words in the box.

a Nǐ .... Yīngyǔ ma?
b Cèsuǒ .... lóuxià.
c Nǐmen .... zài nǎr?
d .... dào lùkǒu.
e Duìbuqǐ, wǒ bù ....
f Nǐ .... shuō Yīngyǔ ma?

zhù	zhīdao
shuō	zǒu
huì	zài

3 Rearrange the following into a conversation.

a Qǐng zài shuō yībiàn.
b Bú kèqì.
c Duìbuqǐ, fùjìn yǒu méi yǒu yínháng?
d Xièxie.
e Zǒu dào hónglǜdēng, wǎng yòu guǎi.
f Zǒu dào hónglǜdēng, wǎng yòu guǎi.
g Qù shì zhōngxīn zěnme zǒu?
h Yínháng zài shì zhōngxīn.

now you're talking!

1 **2•15** You're in a department store and can't see any signs.

- Ask a shopper where the nearest toilet is.
- ◆ **Cèsuǒ zài lóushàng, wǔ céng.**
- Ask her to repeat that.
- ◆ **Cèsuǒ zài lóushàng, wǔ céng.**
- Thank her – and tell your companion in English what she said.

2 **2•16** You get lost on the way back to your hotel.

- Stop a passer-by and ask if he speaks English.
- ◆ **Duìbuqǐ. Bú huì.**
- Ask him how to get to the Zhōngshān Hotel.
- ◆ **Wǎng dōng zǒu, dào dì èr ge hónglǜdēng, wǎng yòu guǎi.**
- Say sorry, you don't understand.
- ◆ **Wǎng dōng zǒu, dào dì èr ge hónglǜdēng, wǎng yòu guǎi, yìzhí zǒu, jiù shì Zhōngshān Fàndiàn.**
- Ask if it's far.
- ◆ **Bù yuǎn, zǒulù shíwǔ fēnzhōng.**

3 **2•17** Later, you get talking to a student staying at the Zhōngshān Hotel.

- Ask him where he lives.
- ◆ **Wǒ zhù zài Xiānggǎng.**
- Ask if his mother and father also live in Hong Kong.
- ◆ **Bù, tāmen zhù zài Shànghǎi. Wǒmen quán jiā dòu zhù zài nàr.**
- Say sorry, you don't understand **quán jiā**.
- ◆ **Quán jiā – bàba hé māma, jiějie, yéye hé nǎinai … wàigōng, wàipó …**
- Now you get it, **quán jiā** means *whole family*. Say you understand.
- ◆ **Nǐ Zhōngwén shuō de hěn hǎo!**
- Accept the compliment modestly – as is the custom in China.

quiz

1 What's the literal meaning of **Dōngjīng**, the Chinese name for Tokyo?

2 Would you expect to see 女 on the women's or the men's toilet?

3 **Xiànchāo jī** means *cashpoint*. What's the difference between **Xiànchāo jī zài nǎr?** and **Zuìjìn de xiànchāo jī zài nǎr?**

4 Should you turn left or right if someone tells you **wǎng zuǒ guǎi?**

5 How might you respond to a compliment?

6 Which is the only verb that doesn't use **bù** for the negative in the present tense?

7 In the UK, what's the equivalent of **shíyī céng?**

8 Given that **gōngzuò** means *to work*, how would you say *I work in Beijing*, and ask *Do you work in Hong Kong?*

Now check whether you can ...

- ask where a place is and how to get there
- follow some basic directions
- ask someone where they live
- say where you and others live
- ask someone to repeat what they've said and to speak more slowly
- check if someone speaks English
- say you speak a little Chinese
- say you don't know or don't understand

Practise what you've just learnt and extend it by using **zài nǎr?** and **zěnme zǒu?** to ask where all the places you learnt in Unit 5 are and how you'd get to them. Then have a go at saying where you and various friends and members of your family live, and whether you speak the languages mentioned on page 55. You could also try writing a paragraph about one particular person, starting with **tā**.

Duōshao qián?

understanding prices in renminbi

asking for what you want

shopping in a department store

bargaining

Zài Zhōngguó ...

shops are open every day, including Chinese New Year, from around 8.30 in the morning until late evening. And you'll find shopping opportunities everywhere, whether from street vendors, **shāngdiàn** and **shìchǎng** selling anything from fresh produce to herbal medicines to silk and cashmere, or exclusive **gòuwù zhōngxīn** *shopping malls* selling international designer labels and exquisite works of art.

In markets and small shops, bargaining over prices is not only acceptable but expected, and payment is in cash. Indeed, away from the big centres, it's a good idea never to assume you can pay by credit card.

Understanding prices in renminbi

Zài Zhōngguó ...

the official currency is **renminbi** (RMB), meaning The People's Currency. There are 3 units: 1 **yuán** = 10 **jiǎo** = 100 **fēn**, although prices in tourist spots tend to be in round **yuán**.

The **yuán** is written ¥, and prices are written with a full stop between **yuán** and the other units: ¥25.75. Informally, **yuán** and **jiǎo** are called **kuài** and **máo**.

1   **2•19** Listen to these prices in renminbi:

¥1.00	**yī yuán**	¥10.30	**shí yuán sān jiǎo**
¥0.10	**yī jiǎo**	¥10.34	**shí yuán sān jiǎo sì fēn**
¥0.01	**yī fēn**	¥50.00	**wǔshí yuán**
¥10.00	**shí yuán**	¥85.75	**bāshíwǔ yuán qī jiǎo wǔ fēn**

2   Now, have a go at saying these prices.

    a   ¥8.00   b   ¥0.87   c   ¥19.50
    d   ¥42.00   e   ¥64.55   f   ¥90.99

3   **2•20** Listen to the key language:

Nín mǎi shénme?   What would you like? *Lit.* you buy what?
.... duōshao qián?   How much is/are the ...? *Lit.* how much money?

4   **2•21** First, get familiar with the names of these fruits. Then listen to people shopping in a **shuǐguǒ diàn** *greengrocer's* and jot down the cost of the various fruits. You'll hear **yī jīn** *per* **jīn** (a **jīn** = 500 grammes).

píngguǒ	**xiāngjiāo**	**lìzhī**	**mángguǒ**	**bōluó**

¥ ....   ¥ ....   ¥ ....   ¥ ....   ¥ ....

Asking for what you want

1 **2•22** Listen to the key language:

Yào duōshao?	How much/many do you want?
Wǒ yào (mǎi) ...	I want (to buy) ...
Wǒ mǎi ...	I'll have *Lit*. I buy ...
... zhè ge/nà ge	... this one/that one
... liǎng ge zhè ge/bā ge nà ge	... 2 of these/8 of those
Hái yào biéde ma?	Would you like anything else?

2 Here's Hannah Cheng's shopping list. Find out what the items are, using the glossary, and work out how they're pronounced.

> fángshàiyóu
> màozi
> míngxìnpiàn
> qiǎokèlì
> lǚyóu dìtú

3 **2•23** Listen to Hannah in the **xiǎomàibù** *corner shop* and note which item she asks for first and what the cost is.

Zài Zhōngwén lǐ ...

yào literally means *want* or *need*, but also conveys the English *would like* in a shopping situation. It can be used with an item or with another verb: **wǒ yào màozi** *I want/need a hat*; **wǒ yào mǎi màozi** *I'd like to buy a hat*. In reply to a question asking if you want/would like something, *Yes* is **Yào** and *No* is **Bú yào**.

---

4 **2•24** Before listening to Hannah asking for the rest of the items, try to anticipate what she might say. When you've listened to the conversation a few times, link each of these phrases with an item from her list, then check with the transcript. Also note how much she spent **yígòng** *altogether*, including the postcards.

- **Wǒ yào ...**
- **Wǒ mǎi zhè ge ...**
- **Yígòng ¥................**
- **Yǒu ... ma?**
- **... duōshao qián?**

Shopping in a department store

1 **2•25** Listen to the key language:

Wǒ zài zhǎo …	I'm looking for …
Wǒ xiǎng kànkan nà ge.	I'd like to have a look at that one.
Wǒ <u>kěyǐ</u> shìshi ma?	<u>May</u> I try it on?
Tài <u>dà/xiǎo</u> le.	It's too <u>big/small</u>.
Yǒu dà/xiǎo hào ma?	Have you got a big/small size?
Yǒu qítā yánsè ma?	Have you got other colours?

Zài Zhōngwén lǐ …

xiǎng is an alternative to yào to convey *would like* when followed by another verb.

Duplicating a verb introduces a casual sense or shorter duration of action: kàn *to look*, kànkan *to have a look*, shì *to try (on)*, shìshi *to have a try*, xiǎng *think*, xiǎngxiang *to think it over*. The repeated verb is unstressed.

---

2 **2•26** Li Guang is at a **bǎihuò shāngdiàn** *department store*, looking for a **lǐngdài** *tie* made of **zhēnsī** *silk* and also a **pījiān** *pashmina* for his girlfriend. The colours available include:

bái(sè) ☐	**hēi(sè)** ■	**hóng(sè)** ■
lán(sè) ■	**lǜ(sè)** ■	**huáng(sè)** ■

Listen to both conversations and make a note in English of the colours he buys.

lǐngdài ....

pījiān ....

> **Shìyījiān zài nǎr?**
> *Where's the changing room?*

3 **2•27** Li Guang then goes to buy a **chènshān** *shirt*. The sizes on offer are:
xiǎo hào *S*, **zhōng hào** *M*, **dà hào** *L*, **jiā dà hào** *XL*

Listen and tick whether these statements are true or false.

	True	False
a He wants a blue shirt	☐	☐
b He tries size medium first	☐	☐
c It's too small for him	☐	☐

Bargaining

1 **2•28** Listen to the key language:

Hěn piàoliang.	(It's/they're) very beautiful.
Tài guì le.	(It's/they're) too <u>expensive</u>.
Piányi yìdiǎn ba?	Can you bring the price down a bit?
Zuìdī jià duōshao?	What's your lowest price? *Lit.* lowest price how much?
... yuán, zěnmeyàng?	How about ... yuan?
Hǎo ba.	Agreed, OK.

2 **2•29** In a **gōngyì měishù diàn** *arts and crafts shop*, Jack falls for a landscape painting and asks his friend Xiaoyue what it's called in Chinese:

- ● **Zhè ge Zhōngwén jiào shénme?**
- ◆ **Shānshuǐ huà.**

They talk to the assistant and Xiaoyue negotiates the price. Listen to their conversation, tick off any of the above key phrases that you hear, and note the price they finally agree on. You'll hear the word **qiān** *thousand*.

¥...................

Zài Zhōngwén lǐ ...

adjectives of one syllable are used as in English: **xiǎo zhēnzhū** *a small pearl*, **dà fēngzheng** *a big kite*; but when the description involves more than one syllable, **de** is added after the adjectives: **piàoliang de zhēnzhū** *a beautiful pearl*; **hěn dà de fēngzheng** *a very big kite*. **Shì** *to be* is not used with adjectives. **G5**

---

3 **2•30** Later, by himself in the market, Jack buys some **zhēnzhū ěrhuán** *pearl earrings* for his girlfriend. Listen and make a note of

a the original asking price ¥......
b how much he ends up paying ¥......

put it **all together**

1   If you buy three items, costing the following amounts, and pay for them all with a ¥100 note, how much change should you expect? How do you say it in Chinese?

èrshí yuán liù jiǎo, jiǔ yuán wǔ jiǎo, sìshíbā yuán yī jiǎo sān fēn

2   Which is the odd one out and why?

a   guì, lán, hóng, hēi, bái
b   xiāngjiāo, qiǎokèlì, bōluó, píngguǒ, lìzhī
c   shuǐguǒ diàn, shāngdiàn, zhēnsī, shìchǎng, gòuwù zhōngxīn
d   piàoliang, zhōng, jiā dà, xiǎo, dà
e   chènshān, lǐngdài, pījiān, màozi, míngxìnpiàn

3   Fill the gaps with the words in the box.

wǒmen	lǜ	ma
mǎi	zhè	shìshi
zhǎo	yǒu	

a   Nín xiǎng .... shénme?
b   Wǒ zài .... chènshān.
c   .... shì zhēnsī chènshān.
d   .... qítā yánsè ....?
e   .... yǒu báisè, lánsè, huángsè, ... sè.
f   Wǒ mǎi lánsè de chènshān. Wǒ kěyǐ .... ma?

4   Rearrange the following to create a dialogue in a market.

a   Duōshao qián?
b   Tài guì le! Piányí yìdiǎn ba?
c   Zhè ge hěn piàoliang.
d   Wǒ yào mǎi fēngzheng.
e   Nín mǎi shénme?
f   Hǎo ba.
g   Èr bǎi yuán, zěnmeyàng?
h   Èr bǎi wǔshí yuán.

What's being bought? How much is it bought for?

1   2•31 Imagine you're visiting Suzhou and doing a bit of shopping. First you want something to eat.

- **Nǐ hǎo. Nǐ mǎi shénme?**
- ◆ You fancy some bananas. Ask how much they are.
- **Sān kuài yī jīn.**
- ◆ Buy 500 grammes of bananas.
- **Hái yào biéde ma?**
- ◆ Point to the pomegranates and say you'll have two of those. Then, in the shop next door, you spot some chocolate. Ask how much it is.
- **Bā yuán wǔ jiǎo.**
- ◆ You missed that. Ask if she'll repeat it.

2   2•32 Now for some presents from the department store.

- **Nín mǎi shénme?**
- ◆ Explain you're looking for a silk tie. Indicate one and add that you'd like to look at this one.
- **Hěn piàoliang de lǐngdài.**
- ◆ Ask if they have it in other colours.
- **Wǒmen yǒu lánsè, hóngsè, lǜsè, huángsè hé.**

3   2•33 Now to the jewellery market where you're going to do a spot of bargaining over a pearl necklace **zhēnzhū xiàngliàn**.

- **Hěn piàoliang de xiàngliàn – dà zhēnzhū. Liǎng qiān liù bǎi yuán.**
- ◆ Tell your friend in English how much it costs. Now tell the seller that it's too expensive.
- **Bú guì!**
- ◆ Ask if they'll bring the price down a bit. Suggest 1,200 yuan.
- **Hǎo ba.**
- ◆ Say thank you, then say goodbye.

quiz

1 How many **jiǎo** are there in a **yuán**? And how many **jīn** in a kilo?

2 What information does **Hái yào biéde ma** ask for?

3 Which of these verbs would you NOT use to say what you want in a shop? **xiǎng, zhù, yào, mǎi, shuō**

4 How would you ask for *five of those*?

5 What size do you think **liǎng ge jiā dà mǎ** is?

6 How do you answer *No* to the following? **Nǐ shì xuésheng ma? Nǐ yào qiǎokèlì ma? Nǐ yǒu háizi ma?**

7 Given that a jacket is **shàngyī** and pure wool is **chúnmáo**, how would you say you're looking for a wool jacket?

8 And if **hòu** means thick, how do you explain that it's too thick?

Now check whether you can ...

- ask how much something costs
- understand the answer in RMB
- ask for an item by name in a shop
- ask for this one/that one; one or more of these/those
- ask if you can have a look at something
- ask if you can try something on
- explain that something is (too) big, small or expensive
- ask for a bigger/smaller size or different colours
- bargain on a price

Word association can double the amount of vocabulary you retain. For example, you could link in your mind words in similar categories, such as **chènshān** and **lǐngdài**, or **míngxìnpiàn** and **yóupiào** *stamps*. When you learn an adjective, learn any obvious opposite as well: **xiǎo** and **dà**, **bái** and **hēi**.

And if you go to China or know any Chinese speakers, make sure you take every opportunity to add to your bank of words by asking ask **Zhè ge Zhōngwén jiào shénme?**

Checkpoint 2

1   **2•34-36** Listen to three people being given directions in their hotel reception. Follow their route on the map and write down in Pinyin and English the place they're going to and the letter which corresponds to it on the map.

a .... b .... c ....

2   Look at the map again, decide if these statements are true or false and correct any false ones. **Jiā** is the measure word for shops, offices, restaurants, etc.

	true	false
a **Yǒu sān jiā jiǔbā.**	☐	☐
b **Méi yǒu gōngyuán.**	☐	☐
c **Bówùguǎn zài shuǐguǒdiàn duìmiàn.**	☐	☐

3 **2•37** The following are foreign words adapted into Chinese. Guess what they mean and check your answers in the glossary.

Then listen and check whether the prices you hear are the same as the ones on the list. Tick the correct ones and change the wrong ones.

1 kǎbùqínuò   ¥15   ☐
2 hànbǎo bāo   ¥31   ☐
1 bǐsà bǐng   ¥24.50   ☐
1 xiāngbīn   ¥97   ☐
1 báilándì   ¥85   ☐
3 wēishìjì   ¥69   ☐

4 Starting with Monday, put these days in order.

> **xīngqītiān**   **xīngqīsì**   **xīngqī'èr**   **xīngqīliù**
>
> **xīngqīyī**   **xīngqīwǔ**   **xīngqīsān**

5 Can you work out what these numbers are? You might like to refer back to pages 26 and 42.

a 十四   **b** 九十   **c** 五十五   **d** 七十三   **e** 六十二

Now see if you can write these in Chinese characters.

f 10   **g** 22   **h** 80   **i** 16

6 Match each sentence to the place in which you're most likely to hear it.

> **shuǐguǒ diàn**   **bówùguǎn**   **fàndiàn**
>
> **jiǔbā**   **bǎihuò shāngdiàn**

a Zhǎnlǎnhuì měi tiān kāimén.
b Cānguǎn zài sì céng.
c Wǒ kéyǐ shìshi zhè jiàn chènshān ma?
d Nǐ hē hóng pútáojiǔ háishì bái pútáojiǔ?
e Wǒ mǎi yī ge mángguǒ hé yī gōngjīn xiāngjiāo.

7 Which of these might you use …

Qǐng zài shuō yībiàn

Duìbuqǐ

Qǐng shuō màn yìdiǎn

Wǒ xiǎng kànkan zhè ge

Kěyǐ shìshi ma?

Tài guì le, piányi yìdiǎn ba

Yǒu dà hào ma?

Nǐ huì shuō Yīngyǔ ma?

a if you want to try something on?
b to find out if someone speaks English?
c if you're looking for a large size?
d when you're bargaining over a price?
e when you'd like to have a look at something in a shop?
f to get someone to speak more slowly?
g to have something repeated?
h to say you're sorry.

8 Put the words below into seven groups, according to meaning. There will be three words in each group.

> dōng   dà   chènshān   shìchǎng   xīcānguǎn
> hǎi biān   jiǔbā   nóngcūn   màozi   xiāngjiāo
> chāojí shìchǎng   lǐngdài   nán   cānguǎn   jiāoqū
> shāngdiàn   guì   běi   píngguǒ   xiǎo   lìzhī

9 Take a close look at the characters for the following **shuǐguǒ** *fruit*.

 苹果 **píngguǒ**   橘子 **júzi**

 芒果 **mángguǒ**   橙子 **chéngzi**

 杨桃 **yángtáo**   桃子 **táozi**

 蜜瓜 **mì guā**   梨子 **lízi**

Now match these characters to their pinyin.

a 椰子   **b** 樱桃   **c** 西瓜   **d** 柠檬

xī guā   **níngméng**   **yēzi**   **yīngtáo**

10 After looking at these characters for various **diàn** *shops*, work out what the ones in the list below them mean in English.

greengrocer's	**shuǐguǒ diàn**	水果店
bakery	**miànbāo diàn**	面包店
grocery shop	**záhuò diàn**	杂货店
flower shop	**huā diàn**	花店
shoe shop	**xié diàn**	鞋店
toy shop	**wánjù diàn**	玩具店
furniture store	**jiājù diàn**	家俱店
bookshop	**shū diàn**	书店
stationery store	**wén jù diàn**	文具店

a 店   **b** 书   **c** 花

d 面包   **e** 鞋   **f** 文具

Yǒu kòng fángjiān ma?

finding a hotel room

... and saying how long you want to stay

checking in

making requests

Zài Zhōngguó ...

there are several words for hotels: **fàndiàn**, **jiǔdiàn**, **bīnguǎn**, and the accommodation available to visitors ranges from **wǔ xīng jí háohuá bīnguǎn** *5-star luxury hotels* to **qīngnián lǚshè** *youth hostels* and **zhāodàisuǒ** *economy guesthouses* – with prices and facilities varying accordingly. The best places for advice and information are the internet and the local **lǚxíngshè** *travel service*.

Large international hotels generally provide both Chinese- and Western-style breakfast, included in the room price. In smaller hotels, you need to check if breakfast is provided and/or included.

Finding a hotel room

1 **2•38** Listen to the key language:

Yǒu (kòng) fángjiān ma?	Is there a room (available)?
Wǒ yào ...	I want ...
... dānrén/shuāngrén/ **liǎngrén fángjiān**	... a single/double/twin room
... dài kōngtiáo	... with air conditioning
... dài yùshì	... with en suite bathroom
Bāo zǎocān ma?	Is breakfast included?

> **Zài Zhōngwén lǐ ...**
>
> fángjiān *room* is often shortened to jiān when coupled with
> dānrén or shuāngrén, e.g. dānrén jiān or even dānjiān. Jiān is also
> the measure word for a room: yī jiān fángjiān, zhè jiān fángjiān.

2 **2•39** Listen to four people enquiring
about rooms at the 3-star Mín Háng
Fàndiàn then, on the grid, tick what kind
of accommodation they want.

Huānyíng guānglín
Welcome

Zhāng Yàn					
Lǐ Míng					
Zhōu Ān					
Chén Hè					

3 **2•40** Listen as Chén Hè goes on to ask about breakfast, and jot down

a in Pinyin the reply to **Bāo zǎocān ma?** What do you think no
would be?

b in English what floor the restaurant is on.

... and saying how long you want to stay

4   2•41 Listen to the key language:

Nín <u>shénme shíhou</u> zhù?	<u>When</u> do you want to stay?
Nín zhù jǐ wǎn?	How many nights do you want to stay?
zhǐ yào jīnwǎn	just for tonight
<u>cóng</u> jīntiān <u>dào</u> xīngqī'èr	<u>from</u> today <u>until</u> Tuesday
Wǒ (yào) zhù ...	I (want to) stay ...
... sān ge wǎnshang/yī ge xīngqī.	... for 3 nights/1 week.
... dào sānyuè liù hào.	... until the 6th of March.
Duìbuqǐ, wǒmen zhù mǎn le.	Sorry, we're full.

5   2•42 Check you understand the following, then listen as people say how long they want their rooms for, numbering the three you hear in the order you hear them.

**wǔ ge wǎnshang..... yī ge xīngqī..... cóng jīntiān dào xīngqīsān .....
zhǐ yào jīnwǎn.......... liǎng ge wǎnshang ......**

Zài Zhōngwén lǐ ...

for the months, you simply put the numbers 1–12 in front of **yuè** *moon, month*:

yīyuè *January*	**èryuè** *February*	**sānyuè** *March*
sìyuè *April*	**wǔyuè** *May*	**liùyuè** *June*
qīyuè *July*	**bāyuè** *August*	**jiǔyuè** *September*
shíyuè *October*	**shíyīyuè** *November*	**shí'èryuè** *December*

The order for dates is: **nián** *year*, **yuè** *month*, **hào** *date*, **tiān** *day of the week*: **èrlínglíngbā nián èryuè shíbā hào xīngqītiān**
Sunday 18 February, 2008

---

6   2•43 The receptionist at the Mín Háng is taking bookings over the phone – you'll hear her say **Wèi** *Hello*, and **Qǐng shāo děng** *One moment, please*. Listen and note when the callers want rooms and which one can't be accommodated.

> **Wèi, nǐ hǎo, shì Mín Háng Fàndiàn**

a .... b .... c ....

Checking in

1 **2•44** Listen to the key language:

Wǒ yùdìng le fángjiān.	I have a reservation.
Nín guì xìng?	Your surname?
Qǐng gěi wǒ nínde hùzhào.	Please give me your passport.
Qǐng tián zhè zhāng biǎo.	Please fill this form.
Qǐng gēn wǒ lái.	Please come with me.
Gěi nín yàoshi.	Here's your key. *Lit*. Give you key.

2 **2•45** Listen to a visitor checking in at the Dōngfāng Hotel and tick the correct option.

a His surname is   Qián   Qíng   Qín   Xíng

b He's booked a   single   double   twin

c He's staying for   1 night   2 nights   4 nights   1 week

d He's asked to   fill in a form   show his passport

e His **fángjiān hàomǎ** *room number* is 617   716   670   706

3 **2•46** Listen to three more people checking in, and note the details of their room on the grid.

			wǎnshang	**fángjiān hàomǎ**
Lǐ xiānsheng				
Zhāng xiǎojie				
Gāo tàitai				

4 Listen again and note where the **diàntī** *lifts* are. ....

Making requests

1   **2•47** Listen to the key language:

Wǒ néng/kěyǐ ... ma?	Can/May I ...
yòng xìnyòngkǎ fù	pay by credit card?
bǎ wǒde xínglǐ liú zài zhèr	leave my luggage here?
Nǐ néng bù néng ...	Can you ...
... liù diǎn jiào xǐng wǒ?	... wake me at 6am?
... gěi wǒ jiào yī liàng chūzūchē?	... call a taxi <u>for</u> me?
Dāngrán kěyǐ.	Of course.

2   **2•48** Wáng Chūn is getting ready to leave the Dōngfāng Hotel. Listen to his conversation with the receptionist Xiǎo Xiá, and note in English the two things he asks her.

a .... b ....

Zài Zhōngwén lǐ ...

as in English, **néng** *can* and **kěyǐ** *may* are used in a similar way:
Wǒ néng yòng xìnyòngkǎ fù ma? *Can I pay by card?* **Wǒ kěyǐ shìshi ma?** *May I try it on?*

To ask somebody else to do something, e.g. wake you at 5 o'clock, you can use **Nǐ néng ... ma?**, **Nǐ néng bù néng ...?** or **Qǐng ...**: **Nǐ néng wǔ diǎn jiào xǐng wǒ ma?**; **Nǐ néng bù néng wǔ diǎn jiào xǐng wǒ?**; **Qǐng wǔ diǎn jiào xǐng wǒ.**

---

3   **2•49** Xiǎo Xiá is kept busy all day with requests from guests. Listen to her at work and number any of the following that you hear.

yòng xìnyòngkǎ fù	
yòng bǎoxiǎnxiāng *use the safe*	
yòng jiànshēnfáng *use the gym*	
yòng hùliánwǎng jiēkǒu *use the internet*	
yòng zhè ge diànhuà *use this phone*	
gěi wǒ jiào yī liàng chūzūchē	
bǎ wǒde xínglǐ liú zài zhèr	

put it all together

Wǒmen zhù	Qǐng	Nǐ néng bù néng	Gěi nǐ
Wǒmen néng ... ma	Wǒ yào	Wǒ kěyǐ ... ma	

1 Which phrase from the box would you use to:

  a say you want or need something,
  b ask someone if they can do something for you,
  c say you (and somebody else) are staying for ...
  d ask if you may do something,
  e hand something over,
  f request someone to do something,
  g ask if you (and somebody else) can ...

2 Complete the following.

  a **Yǒu kòng .... ma?**

  b **Wǒ yào ....**

  c **Wǒ néng yòng........................... ma?**

  d **Nǐ néng bù néng gěi wǒ jiào yī liàng...................**

  e **Qǐng gěi wǒ ....**

3 Say these dates in Chinese:

  a Christmas Day   b New Year's Eve
  c New Year's Day   d St. Valentine's Day

  Now say today's date, including the day of the week and the year, and then say your date of birth.

now you're talking!

1　**2•50** Imagine you're in a hotel in Nanjing, looking for a room for just one night.

- **Huānyíng guānglín. Wǒ néng bāngzhù nǐ ma?** *Can I help you?*
- ◆ Ask if they have a room available.
- **Shuāngrén jiān háishi liǎngrén jiān?**
- ◆ You want a twin room, with a bathroom.
- **Nǐ yào zhù jǐ wǎn?**
- ◆ Answer his question.
- **Yǒu kòng fángjiān.**
- ◆ Ask how much the room costs.
- **Liù bǎi yuán.**
- ◆ Ask if breakfast is included.
- **Bāo zǎocān.**

2　**2•51** Now take the part of Debbie Marshall, arriving at the Dōngfāng Fàndiàn, where she has a room booked for a week.

- Greet the man at reception and say you've got a reservation.
- ◆ **Nín guì xìng?**
- Answer his question.
- ◆ **Dānrén jiān dài kōngtiáo. Sān ge wǎnshang.**
- That's not right. Tell him how long you're staying.
- ◆ **Qǐng shāo děng. Hǎo - yī ge xīngqī. Dào sānyuè liù hào. Qǐng gěi wǒ nínde hùzhào.**
- Hand your passport to him. Say here it is. Now ask if you can pay by credit card.
- ◆ **Dāngrán kěyǐ.**

quiz

1 What do you hand over if you're asked for your **hùzhào**?
2 Which of these is the odd one out? **liǎngrén, Měiguórén, shuāngrén, dānrén**.
3 How do you ask if breakfast is included?
4 Which month comes before **bāyuè**? Which follows it?
5 What is a **chūzūchē**?
6 If you wanted a wake-up call at 7 o'clock, would you say **Nǐ néng bù néng liù diǎn jiào xǐng wǒ?** or **Nǐ néng bù néng qī diǎn jiào xǐng wǒ?**
7 How do you think you say *She wants to stay for 2 weeks* in Chinese?
8 Given that **xǐyīfáng** is a laundry service, how do you ask a) if there's a laundry service, b) if you can use it?

Now check whether you can ...

- say you've booked a room
- ask if there's a room available
- specify whether you want a single, double or twin, with bathroom/air-conditioning
- say how long you want accommodation for, giving precise dates
- ask if you can do something, e.g. pay by credit card
- ask someone else to do something for you

Whenever you take part in a conversation, imagine yourself in that particular situation. What would you expect to hear if you were in a hotel in an English-speaking country, for example? This will help you anticipate what people are going to say – which makes it easier for you to focus and understand what's being said.

Huǒchē jǐ diǎn kāi?

saying where you're going

asking about public transport

finding out train times

... and buying tickets

Zài Zhōngguó ...

chē can refer to anything with wheels if the context makes it clear what's being talked about. If not, you need the full version, ending in **chē**: **qìchē** *car/vehicle*, **gōnggòng qìchē** *bus*, **diànchē** *tram*, **chūzūchē** *taxi*, **zìxíngchē** *bicycle*, **mótuōchē** *motorbike*, **huǒchē** *train*.

In big towns public transport is cheap and frequent, and practically all China's main towns and cities are linked by China Rail – 中国铁路 **Zhōngguó Tiělù** – one of the biggest and busiest networks in the world. Its trains include G-category **gāotiě** *high speed trains* (300km/h); D-category **dòngchē** *speed raised trains* (200–250km/h); Z-category **zhítōngchē** *express (non-stop) fast trains*; T-category **tèkuài** *express fast trains*; K-category **kuàisù** *fast trains*; L-category **línshí lièchē** *temporary passenger trains* and Y-category **línshí lǚyóu lièchē** *temporary tourist trains*. Services are numbered with the category shown by a prefix, e.g. G2581, D331.

Saying where you're going

1 **2•52** Listen to the key language:

Wǒ qù/Wǒ yào qù … I'm going to/I want to go to …
(Nǐ kěyǐ) zuò dìtiě/chūzūchē. (You can) take the underground/
  a taxi.
… huòzhě gōnggòng qìchē. … or a bus.
Nǐ shénme shíhòu qù? When are you going?
jīntiān/míngtiān today/tomorrow

2 **2•53** A visitor to Beijing is asking the hotel receptionist for advice on going to Tiān'ānmén Square. Listen and tick the vehicles you hear mentioned. When does he want to go?

 ....
 ....
 ....

Zài Zhōngwén lǐ …

or is **huòzhě** in a statement and **háishi** in a question: Nǐ kěyǐ zuò chūzūchē huòzhě gōnggòng qìchē *You can take a taxi or a bus*;
Nǐ zuò chūzūchē háishi gōnggòng qìchē? *Are you taking a taxi or a bus?*

---

3 **2•54** Another visitor wants to explore the town centre. Listen and fill the gaps in the conversation with the words from the box. **Dìtú** is a *map*.

> huòzhě   háishi
> shénme shíhou
>   qù   yǒu

- **Wǒ yào ……………… shì zhōngxīn.**
- **Nǐ ………………… qù? Jīntiān ………………… míngtiān?**
- **Míngtiān.**
- **Nǐ kěyǐ zuò dìtiě ……………… chūzūchē.**
- **Hǎo. Nǐ ……………… dìtú ma?**
- **Gěi nǐ.**

Asking about public transport

1   2•55 Listen to the key language:

Yǒu .... (gōnggòng qì)chē ma?	Is there a bus to …?
Zhè ge chē qù … ma?	Does this bus go to …?
Zhè ge chē <u>shénme shíhou</u> kāi?	<u>When</u> does this bus leave?
Zuò jǐ lù chē qù …?	Which number bus goes to …?
Duō jiǔ néng dào?	How long does it take to get there?

Zài Zhōngwén lǐ …

zhōng *clock*, diǎn (zhōng) *o'clock* and fēn(zhōng) *minute* are the key words when talking about time: **wǔ diǎn (zhōng)** *5 o'clock*, **wǔ fēnzhōng** *5 minutes*. **Wǔ fēnzhōng yǐhòu** means *in 5 minutes' time*, and **měi wǔ fēnzhōng** is *every 5 minutes*.

Xiǎoshí means *one hour*, and the number word is **ge**: **liǎng ge xiǎoshí** *two hours*; **měi xiǎoshí** *every hour*, **měi bàn xiǎoshí** *every half an hour*.

2   2•56 Read the names of landmarks found in and around Beijing, listen to passengers making enquiries at **gōnggòng qìchē zǒngzhàn** *the bus station*, and make a note of the information given. Listen out for **yāo**, which is used instead of **yī** *one* in a series of numbers.

- 北海公园 **Běihǎi Gōngyuán** *Beihai Park* ....
- 故宫 **Gù gōng** *The Forbidden City* ....
- 雍和宫 **Yōnghégōng** *The Lama Temple* ....
- 天安门 **Tiān'ānmén** *Tiananmen Square* ....
- 长城 **Chángchéng** *The Great Wall* ....
- 颐和园 **Yíhéyuán** *The Summer Palace* ....

3   Now practise using the key questions in 1 above with the various places, e.g. ask if there's a bus to Tiananmen Square, which number bus goes to the Summer Palace?

Finding out train times

1 **2•57** Listen to the key language:

Jǐ diǎn?	What time?
Huǒchē jǐ diǎn kāi?	What time does the train leave?
Qù Xī'ān de huǒchē jǐ diǎn kāi?	What time does the Xī'an train leave?
Xià yī tàng/bān qù Xī'ān de huǒchē jǐ diǎn kāi?	What time is the <u>next</u> train to Xī'an?
Huǒchē jǐ diǎn dào Xī'ān?	What time does the train arrive in Xī'an?

Zài Zhōngwén lǐ ...

when saying what time things occur, *at* is not translated:

(at) 3.00 **sān diǎn**   (at) 3.20 **sān diǎn èrshí (fēn)**

(at) 3.05 **sān diǎn líng wǔ**   (at) 3.45 **sān diǎn sìshíwǔ (fēn)**

As in English, there are alternatives, e.g. 3.30 can be either **sān diǎn sānshí** or **sān diǎn bàn** *half past three. A quarter past* is **yī kè** and *a quarter to* is **chà yī kè.**

The 24-hour clock is not generally used in everyday speech; **zǎoshang, xiàwǔ** etc. are added when clarification is needed: **Zǎoshang liù diǎn bàn** *6.30 in the morning.*

---

2 **2•58** Listen to people in Beijing station enquiring about trains and fill in the departure time. Note that 2 is **liǎng**, not **èr**, when referring to time.

常州 **Chángzhōu** ....   沈阳 **Shěnyáng** ....

南京 **Nánjīng** ....   秦皇岛 **Qínhuángdǎo** ....

上海 **Shànghǎi** ....

3 **2•59** Listen to another passenger then decide whether the following are true or false.

<table>
<tr><td></td><td></td><td>True</td><td>False</td></tr>
<tr><td>a</td><td>There's a train to Xī'an in half an hour.</td><td>▢</td><td>▢</td></tr>
<tr><td>b</td><td>It leaves at 7.03.</td><td>▢</td><td>▢</td></tr>
<tr><td>c</td><td>It arrives in Xī'an at 6.48am.</td><td>▢</td><td>▢</td></tr>
</table>

...and buying tickets

> **Zài Zhōngguó ...**
>
> the price of train tickets not only reflects a single or return journey
> and the type of train but also the type of seat: 软卧 **ruǎnwò** *soft
> sleeper*, 软座 **ruǎnzuò** *soft seat*, 硬卧 **yìngwò** *hard sleeper*, 硬座
> **yìngzuò** *hard seat*. There's also 站票 **zhàn piào** *standing*.

4   **2•60** Listen to the key language:

Yǒu piào ma?	Are there tickets available?
Wǒ yào mǎi	I want to buy
... yī zhāng piào/liǎng zhāng piào	... 1 ticket/2 tickets
... yī zhāng qù Sūzhōu de piào	... 1 ticket to Suzhou
... yī zhāng dānchéng/wǎngfǎn piào	... 1 single/return ticket
... yī zhāng ruǎnzuò/yìngwò piào ticket	... 1 soft seat/hard sleeper

5   **2•61** Olivia Lam is travelling from Shanghai to Suzhou with friends.
In the ticket office, she's asked **Nǐmen yào mǎi jǐ zhāng piào?** *How
many tickets do you want?* Listen, then fill the gaps in this summary of
what took place.

Lam xiǎojie mǎi .... zhāng .... piào.
Tā yào ruǎnzuò piào.

6   **2•62** Listen to the next passenger then provide the travel information.
You'll hear the train number **Z shísān cì** *Z13*. **Cì** is used for train
numbers, whereas **lù** is used for buses.

destination ....   dep. time ....   arr. time ....
ticket ....   seat ....   ¥ ....

售票处
Shòupiàochù
ticket office

put it all together

1 Match the times to the clocks.

1 `02.25`   2 `10.05`   3 `08.35`

4 `01.15`   5 `03.50`   6 `05.10`

a Yī diǎn shíwǔ   b bā diǎn sānshíwǔ
c liǎng diǎn èrshíwǔ   d shí diǎn líng wǔ
e wǔ diǎn shí fēn   f sān diǎn wǔshí

2 Say these times in Chinese, using *quarter/half* where appropriate. You might need to refer to page 82.

a 7.30am   b 6.23pm
c 12.15pm   d 10.40am
e 4.05pm   f 4.45am

3 Which is the odd one out and why?

a zǎoshang , zǎocān, zhōngwǔ, wǎnshang, shàngwǔ
b zìxíngchē, tèkuàichē, pǔtōngchē, pǔkuàichē, huǒchē
c míngtiān, xiànzài, jīntiān, jīnwǎn, píngguǒ
d hùzhào, ruǎnzuò, yìngzuò, ruǎnwò, yìngwò
e xiǎoshí, diǎn, fēn, zhōng, piào

4 Rearrange the words to discover three questions related to travel. What do they mean?

a gōnggòng qìchē   ma   Chángchéng   yǒu
  de   qù

b Běijīng   qù   nǐ   shénme shíhou

c huǒchē   jǐ diǎn   Nánjīng de   kāi
  xià yī tàng   qù

now you're talking!

1　**2·63** You're with a friend at a **gōnggòng qìchē zhàn** in Beijing, on your way to the **Yíhéyuán** *Summer Palace*.

- Ask the woman in the office if there's a bus to the Summer Palace.
- ◆ **Yǒu. Qīshíbā lù chē. Měi shí fēnzhōng yī tàng.**
- Tell your friend what number bus it is and how often they go. Now find out how long it takes to get there.
- ◆ **Èrshíwǔ fēnzhōng.**
- Ask how much a ticket costs.
- ◆ **Shíliù yuán.**
- Say you want to buy two tickets.
- ◆ **Gěi nǐ.**
- Thank her.
- ◆ **Bú xiè.**

2　**2·64** Now you're off to Xī'an by train on your own.

- Ask the man in the ticket office what time the next train leaves.
- ◆ **Liù diǎn sìshíwǔ fēn.**
- Find out what time the train arrives in Xī'an.
- ◆ **Zǎoshang qī diǎn líng wǔ.**
- Say you'd like a ticket.
- ◆ **Dānchéng háishi wǎngfǎn?**
- You want a single.
- ◆ **Nǐ yào ruǎnzuò piào ma?**
- It's a long journey. Say you want a soft sleeper and ask the price.
- ◆ **Liùshí'èr yuán. Gěi nǐ. Yí lù píng ān.** *Bon voyage!*

quiz

1 Is **jiǔ diǎn chā yī kè** 9.15 or 8.45? What would 9.30 be?
2 What would you be waiting for at a **gōnggòng qìchē zhàn**?
3 Why would you go to a **shòupiàochù**?
4 Would you use **háishi** or **huòzhě** to mean or in a question?
5 What kind of train is a **tèkuài lièchē**? What prefixes the train number?
6 Is a **yìngzuò** or a **ruǎnwò** likely to be more comfortable? What is **zhàn piào**?
7 What's the difference between **měi bàn xiǎoshí** and **bàn xiǎoshí yǐhòu**?
8 Given that **guānmén** means to close, how would you ask what time the bank closes?

Now check whether you can ...

- say where you're going/want to go
- ask if there's a bus going to a particular place
- find out when it leaves
- ask how long it takes to get to a place
- ask what time a train departs and arrives
- understand the time of day
- buy a ticket, single or return, for various seats

On the internet there's a wealth of information about **Zhōngguó Tiělù** China Rail, including detail of timetables, ticket prices, etc. Using it to plan a hypothetical journey will bring to life what you've just learnt – work out what questions you'd need to ask to buy tickets for particular seats, and to find out what time trains leave and what time they arrive at their destination. **Yí lù píng ān!**

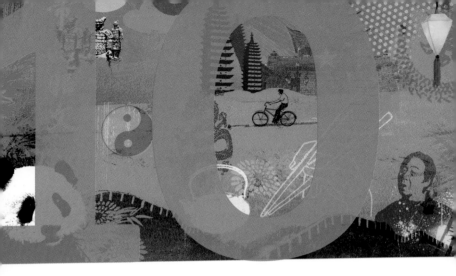

Mànmàn chī

choosing a place to eat

understanding what's on the menu

ordering a meal

expressing appreciation

Zài Zhōngguó ...

most eating places serve breakfast, lunch and dinner; in-between some also serve **diǎnxīn** *snacks* (**dímsum** in Cantonese). **Chá** is traditionally served with meals, but soft drinks, **píjiǔ** and **pútáojiǔ** are also popular now.

There are eight major regional cuisines: **yuècài** *Cantonese/Guangdong* (exotic ingredients, light, mild), **lǔcài** *Shandong* (seafood, peanuts, shallots/garlic seasoning), **mǐncài** *Fujian* (seafood, tasty, pickled ingredients) **jiāngsūcài** *Jiangsu* (fish/crustaceans, delicate, sweet), **zhècài** *Zhejiang* (smooth, mellow), **huīcài** *Anhui* (slow-cooked braised dishes). **chuāncài** *Sichuan/Szechuan* and **xiāngcài** *Hunan* make much use of chilli, garlic, ginger and pepper and can be very **là** *hot/spicy*.

Choosing a place to eat

1 **2•65** Listen to the key language:

Wǒmen wǎnshang chī shénme?	What shall we eat tonight?
Wǒmen chī ..., hǎo bù hǎo?	What if we eat ...?
Wǒ (bù) xǐhuan ...	I (don't) like ...
Wǒ hěn xǐhuan	I really like ...
Wǒ gèng xǐhuan ...	I prefer ...
Hǎo zhǔyi	Good idea

2 **2•66** Listen to Haijiao and some friends discussing where to eat, and tick the key phrases as you hear them. Do they decide on one of these or on **jiǎozi** dumplings?

chuāncài	**huīcài**	**lǔcài**	**mǐncài**
jiāngsūcài	**xiāngcài**	**yuècài**	**zhècài**

Zài Zhōngwén lǐ ...

hěn means *very* with adjectives and *very much/really* with verbs:

Chuāncài hěn là. *Sichuan food is <u>very</u> spicy.*

Wǒ hěn xǐhuān chuāncài. *I like Sichuan food <u>very much</u>.*

---

3 **2•67** As they enter the restaurant, they're asked **Nǐmen jǐ wèi?** *How many of you are there? Lit. You how many people?* The MW **wèi** is used instead of the standard **ge** to show extra politeness to customers in shops and restaurants.

Listen as they and another party are greeted, and note how many people there are in each group: **a** .... **wèi** **b** .... **wèi**

4 **2•68** Listen as they're given the **càidān** *menu* and asked what they want to drink **Nǐmen xiǎng hē shénme?** Which of these do they choose?

píjiǔ	**hóng pútáojiǔ**	**chá**	**mǐjiǔ** *rice wine*
	bái pútáojiǔ	**kuàngquán shuǐ**	

Understanding what's on the menu

1   Have a look at the following:

> **yú** *fish*   **hǎixiān** *seafood*   **xiā** *shrimp*   **dàxiā** *prawns*   **lóngxiā** *lobster*
> **ròu** *meat*   **niúròu** *beef*   **zhūròu** *pork*   **yángròu** *lamb*
> **páigǔ** *spare ribs*   **jī(ròu)** *chicken*   **jīdàn** *eggs*   **yā** *duck*   **dòufu** *tofu*
>
> **shícài/qīngcài** *seasonal/green vegetables*   **bōcài** *spinach*
> **báicài** *Chinese leaves*   **jièlán** *Chinese broccoli*
> **dòuyá** *beansprouts*   **xīhóngshì** *tomato*   **mógu** *mushroom*
> **cōng** *onion*   **suàn** *garlic*
>
> **mǐfàn** *rice*   **bái (mǐ)fàn** *boiled* (lit. *white*) *rice*   **dàn chǎo fàn** *egg-fried*
> *rice*   **miàn(tiáo)** *noodles*   **bāozi** *steamed bun*   **jiǎozi** *dumplings*
>
> **jiān** *fried*   **zhá** *deep fried*   **chǎo** *stir fried/sautéed*   **kǎo** *roasted*
> **lǔshuǐ** *marinated*   **qīngzhēng** *steamed*   **gālí** *curry*   **tángcù** *sweet*
> *and sour lit. sugar vinegar*   **suānlà** *hot and sour lit. sour hot*

2   Now work out what these dishes are.

> ### 汤 **Tāng** *Soups*
>
> 鱼汤 **yú tāng**   酸辣汤 **suānlà tāng**
>
> ---
>
> ### 主食 **Zhǔshí** *Staple carbohydrates*
>
> 白米饭 **bái mǐfàn**   蛋炒饭 **dàn chǎofàn**
> 炒面 **chǎomiàn**
>
> ---
>
> ### 主菜 **Zhǔcài** *Main courses*
>
> 糖醋鸡 **tángcù jī**   炒羊肉 **chǎo yángròu**
> 北京烤鸭 **Běijīng kǎoyā**   咖哩牛肉 **gālí niúròu**
> 卤水豆腐 **lǔshuǐ dòufu**   糖醋排骨 **tángcù páigǔ**
> 时菜 **shícài**   炒芥兰蘑菇 **chǎo jièlán mógu**

Ordering a meal

1 **2•69** Listen to the key language:

Qǐng lái ...	Please bring ...
... yī ge gālí jīròu	... 1 chicken curry
... yī zhī kǎoyā	... 1 roast duck
... yī wǎn mǐfàn	... 1 bowl of rice
Wǒmen dōu yào ...	We both/all want ...
... là bú là?	Is the ... spicy?

2 **2•70** First work out what these two questions mean, then listen as Haijiao starts ordering and jot down his order. You'll hear **nàme** *in that case/then so*.

Zhǔcài yào shénme?
Zhǔshí yào shénme?

Nǐmen diǎn cài ma?
Are you ready to order?

3 **2•71** Haijiao's Australian friend Amanda talks to the waitress about an item on the menu. Before listening, read their conversation and work out what **chīsù** means. What does she order?

- **Wǒ bù chī ròu – wǒ chīsù. Zhè ge cài yǒu méi yǒu ròu?**
- **Yǒu. Nín chī dàn ma?**
- **Bù chī dàn. Lǚshuǐ dòufu là bú là?**
- **Bú là, bú là.**
- **Nàme, qǐng lái yī ge lǚshuǐ dòufu, xièxie.**

Zài Zhōngguó ...

at the start of a meal, you might be told **Mànmàn chī** which literally means *Slowly slowly eat*, in other words, *Take your time and enjoy your meal*. An alternative is **Màn yòng**. **Gān bēi** traditionally expects you to empty your glass, although it's increasingly used simply as *Cheers*.

---

4 **2•72** As the meal is served, Haijiao calls the **fúwùyuán** (the word for both *waiter* and *waitress*). What does he order to drink? He asks for something else – **zái lài** *as well*. Is it:

chāzi **kuàizi** or **sháozi?**

Expressing appreciation

1 **2•73** Listen to the key language:

Gòu ma?	Is that enough?
Gòu le.	That's enough.
Nǐ chī bǎo le ma?	Are you full?
Wǒ chī bǎo le.	I'm full.
Fàncài hěn hǎochī.	The food is/was delicious.
Qǐng jiézhàng/mǎidān.	The bill, please.

2 **2•74** The waitress asks **Hái yào biéde ma?** *Anything else?* and Haijiao checks with his friends. Listen and make a note of how they reply.

Tíng Huá ....

Jiàn Zhōng ....

Amanda ....

> **Zài Zhōngwén lǐ ...**
>
> **le**, which doesn't translate into English, has several functions, including:
>
> - showing a change of state: **wǒ chī bǎo le** *I'm full* (whereas I wasn't before);
> - meaning *extremely*, when used with **tài** and an adjective: **tài hǎo le** *extremely good*. Another way of saying *extremely* is **fēicháng**.   **G12**

3 **2•75** The waitress then asks if they enjoyed their meal **Fàncài zěnmeyàng?** Listen as they reply and add the compliments.

- **Fàncài zěnmeyàng?**
- ◆ .... **xièxie.**
- **Kǎoyā ...., ...!**
- ◆ **Qǐng jiézhàng.**
- **Qǐng shāo děng. Gěi nín.**
- ◆ **Jīntiān wǒ qǐngkè.** *Today it's my treat.*
- **Xièxie.**
- ◆ **Zàijiàn!**

put it all together

1 Put these in the order you're most likely to hear them in a restaurant.

   a **Zhǔshí yào shénme?**   b **Xièxie. Zàijiàn!**
   c **Nǐmen xiǎng hē shénme?**   d **Zhǔcài yào shénme?**
   e **Zhè shì zhàngdān.**   f **Fàncài zěnmeyàng?**
   g **Qǐng wèn, nǐmen jǐ wèi?** h **Zhè shì càidān.**

2 Which of these would you use

   wǒ bù chī yú

   wǒ hěn xǐhuan yú

   yú tài hǎo le

   wǒ gèng xǐhuan yú

   zhè ge yú là ma

   wǒ bù xǐhuan yú

   a if you don't like fish?   b to say you don't eat fish?
   c to say you prefer fish?   d when you really like fish?
   e when the fish is extremely   f to ask if this fish is spicy?
      good?

3 What are these dishes?

   a **hǎixiān tāng**   b **niúròu tāng**
   c **tángcù zhūròu**   d **chǎo qīngcài dòufu**
   e **gālí yángròu**   f **zhá dàxiā**
   g **xīhóngshì jīdàn tāng**   h **jiān dàn**

4 In Chinese, how would you

   a say you like Cantonese food?
   b ask someone if he likes rice wine?
   c say you prefer beer?
   d say you both really like **Zhōngcān** Chinese food?

1   2•76 Imagine you're in a restaurant in Beijing with a friend who doesn't speak Chinese. You're greeted by the waitress.

- **Huānyíng guānglín. Qǐng wèn, jǐ wèi.**
- ◆ Say there are two of you.
- **Qǐng zuò. Nǐmen yào hē shénme?**
- ◆ Say you'll both drink tea please.
- **Zhè shì càidān.**
- ◆ Thank her.

She returns a few minutes later.
- **Nǐmen diǎncài ma?**
- ◆ Ask for one stir-fried beef and a Beijing roast duck.
- **Zhǔshí yào shénme?**
- ◆ Order a bowl of boiled rice and a bowl of noodles.
- **Nǐmen yào kuàizi háishi chāzi?**
- ◆ She's asking if you want chopsticks or forks. Go for the chopsticks.

When she brings the food ...
- **Gěi nín – yī ge chǎo niúròu hé yī zhī kǎoyā, mǐfàn, miàntiáo. Hái yào biéde ma?**
- ◆ Ask her to bring two bottles of beer.
- **Hǎo. Mànmàn chī.**

When you've finished ...
- **Fàncài zěnmeyàng?**
- ◆ Say the food was delicious.
  Now ask for the bill.
- **Qǐng shāo děng.**

quiz

1 Going into a restaurant, how would you say there are four of you?

2 Would **hóngshāo yángròu** be suitable for a vegetarian?

3 How do you attract the attention of the waiter or waitress?

4 Which is the odd one out? **dòuyá, dàxiā, hǎixiān, yú, lóngxiā.**

5 If **Zhōngcān** is *Chinese food*, what do you think **Xīcān** is?

6 What's the difference between a) **Zhǔshí yào shénme?** and b) **Zhǔshí yǒu shénme?**

7 How would you find out if **yú xiāng niúròu** is spicy?

8 Given that nuts are **guǒrén**, how would you ask if **gālí niúròu** has nuts in it?

Now check whether you can ...

- understand the Chinese for basic menu items
- order a meal, main course and staple, and a drink
- say what you like, don't like and prefer
- pay a compliment on the food
- ask for the bill
- offer to pay for the meal

Now get ready for the final Checkpoint, which covers the whole of **Talk Mandarin Chinese**, with a bit of revision. Listen to the conversations again, test your knowledge of the key language by covering up the English and the Chinese in turn, and use the quizzes and checklists at the end of each unit to assess how much you remember.

Checkpoint 3

Imagine you've just arrived in China on holiday ...

1   It's Sunday. Tired and thirsty, you arrive at Beijing's rail station, and look for the nearest bar. Which of these questions would you ask?

   a   **Duìbuqǐ, yǒu cānguǎn ma?**
   b   **Duìbuqǐ, jiǔbā jīntiān kāimén ma?**
   c   **Duìbuqǐ, zuìjìn de jiǔbā zài nǎr?**
   d   **Duìbuqǐ, shìchǎng zài nǎr?**

2   Having found a bar, you order a drink.

   ● **Nín hǎo. Nín hē shénme?**
   ◆ A bottle of beer ………………………......................
   ● **Xiǎo de háishi dà de?**
   ◆ A large one please. …………………….................
   ● How much is it? …………………………….........
   ◆ **Èrshísì yuán.**

   Note down in words how much change you'd expect from a 100 **yuán** note.

3   After your drink, how would you ask the waiter   **Qǐng wèn ...**

   a   where the toilet is?
   b   if there's an internet café nearby?
   c   whether the post office is open today?
   d   how to get to the Xin Gang Wan Hotel?

4   2•77 Listen to his reply to the last question and make a note in English of the directions you're given.

5   Before leaving the station, you want to find out what time there's a train for Dalian on Thursday, what time it arrives and how much a return ticket costs. For each question, choose the correct options.

    a   Xīngqīyī/xīngqīsì qù Dàlián de huǒchē/chūzūchē jǐ diǎn kāi?

    b   Huǒchē jǐ diǎn zài/dào Dàlián?

    c   Duōshao qián yī zhāng wǎngfǎn/dānchéng piào?

6   You've already booked an en suite room at the Xin Gang Wan Hotel for a week. At reception which of the following would you say?

    a   Wǒ yùdìng le sān wǎnshang dānrén jiān dài yùshì.
    b   Wǒ xiǎng yào dài kōngtiáo de fángjiān, cóng jīntiān dào xīngqīsì.
    c   Yǒu kòng dānrén jiān dài yùshì qī ge wǎnshang ma?
    d   Wǒ yùdìng le yī ge xīngqī de dānrén jiān dài yùshì.

7   2•78 Listen to the receptionist's reply. Make a note in English of the two things she asks you, your room number and where the lift is.

    a   ....
    b   ....
    c   ....
    d   ....

8   2•79 In the evening you go looking for a birthday present for your sister. Listen to the audio and take part in a conversation in a shop selling **pí** *leather*. You'll need to be able to say:

    • I want to buy a **shǒutíbāo** *handbag*.
    • It's too big.
    • Can I have a look at that one?
    • I really like it.
    • How much is it?
    • It's too expensive.
    • How about 800 yuan?
    • Can I pay by credit card?

9 Later in the hotel bar, you get talking to Tanaka Keiko, who's Japanese, from Tokyo.

How would she answer these questions?

a **Nǐ jiào shénme?**
b **Nǐ shì bú shì Zhōngguórén?**

10 2•80 What questions would you need to have asked Keiko if these are her replies?

a ....
● **Wǒ zhù zài Dōngjīng.**
b ....
● **Wǒ shì gōngchéngshī.**
c ....
● **Wǒ jiéhūn le.**
d ....
● **Wǒ yǒu yī ge érzi.**
e ....
● **Tā jiǔ suì.**
f ....
● **Wǒ huì shuō yìdiǎn Yīngwén. Nǐ Zhōngwén shuō de zhēn hǎo!**
g ....
● **Xǐhuan – wǒ hěn xǐhuan Běijīng cài. Fēicháng hǎo!**

She now asks you about yourself. Listen to the audio and answer her.

11 2•81 Listen to Keiko's plans for the week and note in the diary when she'll be in Beijing, Dalian and Jinzhou and when she's returning to Japan. As in English, the present tense of verbs is used for the future when the context makes it clear when things are happening.

> **dāi** to stay
> **dào** to arrive
> **zhídào** until

Mon		**Fri**	
....		....	
Tues		**Sat**	
....		....	
Wed		**Sun**	
....		....	
Thur			
....			

12 Later, Keiko helps you to decipher the menu in the hotel restaurant. First have a look at these characters for ingredients you know.

鱼 yú   肉 ròu
大虾 dàxiā   羊肉 yángròu
鸡 jī   牛肉 niúròu
鸭 yā   猪肉 zhūròu
豆腐 dòufu

Now use the above ingredients as the key to match the following.

a	鱼香牛肉	1	**Běijīng kǎoyā** *Beijing roast duck*
b	油焖大虾	2	**dòufu shāo yú** *fried fish with tofu*
c	豆腐烧鱼	3	**qīngzhēng quánjī** *steamed whole chicken*
d	北京烤鸭	4	**yú xiāng niúròu** *Yu-Shiang spicy garlic beef*
e	清蒸全鸡	5	**yóumèn dàxiā** *braised prawns*

Finally, identify the main ingredient of these dishes (Pinyin and English on page 89).

f 牛肉炖土豆 ....

g 啤酒鸡 ....

h 烤羊腿 ....

i 野菌烧豆腐 ....

j 豆腐烧鱼 ....

k 砂锅鱼头 ....

l 猪肉炖粉条 ....

m 干锅鸡 ....

n 西湖醋鱼 ....

o 涮羊肉 ....

Liǎobuqǐ *Congratulations*. You've reached the end of **Talk Mandarin Chinese**. Be prepared to hear **Nǐ Zhōngwén shuō de zhēn hǎo** and to reply modestly **Nǎli nǎli!**

transcripts and answers

This section contains the scripts of all the **Talk Mandarin Chinese** conversations. Answers which consist of words/phrases from the conversations are in bold type; other answers are given separately.

Unit 1

Pages 8-9 Saying hello and goodbye

2 ● Nǐ hǎo.
  ◆ Nǐ hǎo.
  ● Luó Píng, nǐ hǎo ma?
  ◆ **Hěn hǎo**, xièxie.
  She's very well.

3 ● Nǐ hǎo.
  ◆ Nín hǎo.
  ● Nǐ hǎo ma?
  ◆ Wǒ hěn hǎo, xièxie.
  ● Nǐmen hǎo.
  ◆ Nǐ hǎo.
  ● Nǐmen hǎo ma?
  ◆ Wǒmen hěn hǎo, xièxie.
  ● Wáng Wěiléi, nǐ hǎo ma?
  ◆ Mǎmǎhūhū. Nǐ ne?
  ● Hěn hǎo, xièxie.
  She greets a single person first. You hear xièxie 3 times.

4 ● Fàn Yǒng, **zǎoshang hǎo**.
  ◆ Luó Píng, **zǎoshang hǎo**.
  ● Wú Lán, **nǐ hǎo**.
  ◆ Nǐ hǎo.
  ● Lǐ xiānsheng, **wǎnshang hǎo**.
  ◆ Wǎnshang hǎo.
  ● Wáng Yuányuan, **nǐ hǎo**.
  ◆ Luó Píng, nǐ hǎo.
  ● Chén Jiàntāo, **zǎoshang hǎo**.
  ◆ Zǎoshang hǎo.

6 ● Lǐ xiānsheng, **míngtiān jiàn**.
  ◆ Zhào Mǐn, **huítóu jiàn**.
  ● Chén tàitai, **zàijiàn**.
  ◆ Lǐ Yǒng, **wǎn'ān**. **Míngtiān jiàn**.
  ● Zhào Wěiléi, **wǎnshang jiàn**.

7 ● Zàijiàn, zàijiàn.
  ◆ Zàijiàn, Tíngtíng, **míngtiān jiàn**.
  ● Léilei, **wǎnshang jiàn**.

  Tíngtíng: **míngtiān jiàn** *tomorrow*;
  Léilei: **wǎnshang jiàn** *this evening*.

8 bǎi; è; sī; wō; wǔ; yù
  chá; chē; běi; xī; wò; lù; yǔ

Pages 10-11 Introducing yourself and getting to know people

2 ● Duìbuqǐ, nín shì Chén xiānsheng ma?
  ◆ Wǒ bú shì.
  ● Nín shì Chén xiānsheng ma?
  ◆ Wǒ bú shì.
  ● Duìbuqǐ, nín shì Chén xiānsheng ma?
  ◆ Shìde, wǒ shì.

3 ● Nǐ shì Gāo Zǐxiáng xiānsheng ma?
  ◆ Bú shì, wǒ shì **Gāo Zhìqiáng**.

4 ● Nǐ shì Zhōng xiǎojie ma?
  ◆ Wǒ bú shì.
  ● Wǒ shì + *your name*.

6 ● **Wǒ jiào** Zhào Zhōuzhou.
  ◆ Hěn gāoxìng rènshi nǐ.

7 ● Nǐ hǎo. Nǐ xìng shénme? Nǐ shì Wáng xiānsheng ma?
  ◆ Bú shì. Wǒ xìng **Huáng**. Wǒ jiào **Huáng Xuě**.
  ● Nín hǎo, Huáng xiānsheng, hěn gāoxìng rènshi nín.
  ◆ Wǒ yě hěn gāoxìng rènshi nǐ.

8 ● **Zǎoshang** hǎo. **Nín** shì Wáng Hǎiqìng xiānsheng **ma**?
  ◆ Shì, **wǒ** shì.
  ● Wǒ **shì** Lǐ Xiǎoyuè. **Hěn** gāoxìng rènshi nín.

Page 12 Put it all together

1 *a* Nǐ jiào shénme?; *b* Nǐ hǎo; *c* Wǒ jiào; *d* Duìbuqǐ; *e* Wǎnshang hǎo; *f* Wǒ bú shì; *g* Wǎn'ān; *h* Wǒ hěn hǎo,

xièxie; *i* Hěn gāoxìng rènshi nǐ.
Nǐ hǎo ma? *(How are you?)* is left
over.

2 *1* Nǐ hǎo.
  2 Zǎoshang hǎo.
  3 Nǐmen hǎo.
  4 Zàijiàn.

Page 13 Now you're talking!

1 • **Nǐ hǎo.**
  ◆ Zǎoshang hǎo. Nǐ xìng shénme?
  • **Wǒ xìng Newman.**
  ◆ Shì Jake Newman xiānsheng ma?
  • **Shìde, wǒ shì Jake Newman.**
    Duìbuqǐ, tā shì Gǒng Lì ma?
  ◆ Shìde, tā shì Gǒng Lì.

2 • Zǎoshang hǎo. Wǒ shì Huáng Nà.
    Nǐ jiào shénme?
  ◆ **Wǒ shì Jake Newman.**
  • Hěn gāoxìng rènshi nǐ.
  ◆ **Hěn gāoxìng rènshi nǐ, Huáng Nà.**
  • **Huáng Nà, zàijiàn.**
  ◆ Míngtiān jiàn.

3 • Gāo Wénpíng, wǎnshang hǎo.
  ◆ **Wǎnshang hǎo.**
  • Nǐ hǎo ma?
  ◆ **Mǎmǎhūhū. Nǐ ne?**
  • Wǒ hěn hǎo, xièxie.

Page 14 Quiz

1 *1* when greeting more than
one person; *2* **hěn hǎo, xièxie,
mǎmǎhūhū**; *3* **wǎnshang hǎo** *good
evening*, **wǎnshang jiàn** *see you
this evening*, **míngtiān wǎnshang**
tomorrow evening; *4* what his/her
name is; *5* when you first meet
somebody; *6* **shì/shìde** *yes*, **bú shì**
no; *7* a married woman; *8* **xīngqīliù
jiàn**.

Unit 2

Pages 16 & 17 Talking about nationality and where you come from

2 • Duìbuqǐ, nǐ shì nǎ guó rén?
  ◆ Wǒ shì Xīnxīlánrén.

• Nǐ shì nǎ guó rén?
◆ Wǒ shì Yīngguórén.
• Duìbuqǐ, nǐ shì Měiguórén ma?
◆ Bú shì, wǒ shì Jiānádàrén.
• Nǐ ne?
◆ Wǒ shì Yīngguórén.
• Nǐ shì nǎ guó rén?
◆ Wǒ shì Xīnxīlánrén.
*1 Xīnxīlánrén; 2 Yīngguórén;
3 Jiānádàrén; 4 Yīngguórén;
5 Xīnxīlánrén*

3 Zhōngguó Zhōngguórén; Hánguó
Hánguórén; Rìběn Rìběnrén;
Yīnggélán Yīnggélánrén; Sūgélán
Sūgélánrén; Wēi'ěrshì Wēi'ěrshìrén;
Àodàlìyà Àodàlìyàrén; Ài'ěrlán
Ài'ěrlánrén.

6 • Nǐ cóng nǎr lái? **Wǒ cóng Ài'ěrlán
    lái.**
  ◆ Nǐ ne? **Wǒ shì Àodàlìyàrén, wǒ
    cóng Xīní lái.**
  • Nǐ yě shì Àodàlìyàrén ma? **Bú shì,
    wǒ cóng Lúndūn lái.**
  ◆ Nǐ cóng nǎr lái? **Wǒ cóng Měiguó
    lái, cóng Niǔyuē lái.**
  • Nǐ shì běndìrén ma? **Shìde, wǒ shì
    Shànghǎirén.**
  ◆ Nǐ yě shì Shànghǎirén ma? **Bù.
    Wǒ shì Nánjīngrén … wǒ cóng
    Nánjīng lái.**

7 • Nǐ hǎo. Nǐ jiào shénme?
  ◆ Wǒ jiào Hannah.
  • Nǐ cóng nǎr lái?
  ◆ Wǒ shì Yīngguórén – wǒ cóng
    Lánkǎisītè lái.
  • Wǒ jiào Mark … Wǒ jiào Susie.
  ◆ Hěn gāoxìng rènshi nǐmen. Nǐmen
    cóng nǎr lái?
  • Wǒmen shì Àodàlìyàrén – wǒmen
    cóng **Kānpéilā** lái.

Page 18 Saying what you do for a living

2 • Nǐ zuò shénme gōngzuò?
  ◆ Wǒ shì **dǎoyóu.**
  • Nǐ zuò shénme gōngzuò?

- Wǒ shì **lǎoshī**.
- Xiānsheng, nǐ ne?
- Wǒ shì **lǜshī**.
- Xáojie, nǐ shì xuésheng ma?
- Bù, wǒ shì **yīshēng**.
- Nǐ yě shì yīshēng ma?
- Bù, wǒ shì **fúwùyuán**.
- Nín zuò shénme gōngzuò?
- Wǒ shì **jìzhě**.
- Wǒ shì **gōngchéngshī**.

1 tour guide; 2 teacher; 3 lawyer;
4 doctor; 5 waiter; 6 journalist;
7 engineer.

3 • Bāo Yúntiān shì yīshēng. Tā zài
    yīyuàn gōngzuò. Liú Chàng shì
    gōngchéngshī. Tā zài Shànghǎi yī
    jiā gōngchǎng gōngzuò. Cài Xuán
    zài bàngōngshì gōngzuò. Tā shì
    kuàijìshī.
  • Lín Jiājia ne?
  • Tā zài dàxué xué Yīngwén.

Bāo Yúntiān: doctor/hospital; Liú
Chàng: engineer/factory in Shanghai;
Cài Xuán: accountant/office; Lín Jiājia:
studies English/University.

Page 19 Giving your phone number

2 bā, sān, wǔ, sì, shí, líng, liù, yī, qī, jiǔ,
  èr.

4 • Nǐde diànhuà hàomǎ shì shénme?
  • Wǒde shǒujī hàomǎ shì líng qī qī èr
    liù líng bā bā líng jiǔ bā. Wǒ jiā de
    diànhuà hàomǎ shì líng yāo wǔ èr
    sì bā jiǔ èr wǔ líng líng. Wǒ gōngsī
    de diànhuà hàomǎ shì líng líng sì sì
    yāo qī qī èr bā jiǔ èr jiǔ líng jiǔ.
Home no: 01524 892 500;
Work no: 00 44 1772 892 909.

Page 20 Put it all together

1 *a* Bù, wǒ shì Sūgélánrén; *b* Shì, wǒ shì
  Měiguórén; *c* Shì qī bā sān wǔ bā jiǔ;
  d Wǒ shì gōngchéngshī; *e* Bú shì, wǒ
  shì jìzhě; *f* Wǒ cóng Sūgélán lái.

2 xìng: Yú; guójí: Zhōngguórén; zhíyè:
  yīshēng; diànhuà hàomǎ: 010
  85509166

3 Wǒ **xìng** Liáng. Wǒ **jiào** Liáng Hǎijiāo.
  Wǒ shì Guǎngzhōurén, wǒ **cóng**
  Guǎngzhōu **lái**. Wǒ zài **yínháng**
  gōngzuò, wǒ shì **lǜshī**.

4 Wǒ xìng Huáng. Wǒ jiào Huáng
  Méilíng. Wǒ shì Zhōngguórén,
  wǒ cóng Xiānggǎng lái. Wǒ zài
  bàngōngshì gōngzuò, wǒ shì kuàijìshī.

  Wǒ xìng Daniels. Wǒ jiào Rhodri. Wǒ
  shì Wēi'ěrshìrén, wǒ cóng Bangor lái.
  Wǒ zài dàxué gōngzuò, wǒ shì lǎoshī.

Page 21 Now you're talking!

1 • Pí'ěrsūn xiǎojie, nǐ shì Měiguórén
    ma?
  • **Bú shì, wǒ shì Yīngguórén.**
  • Nǐ cóng nǎr lái?
  • **Wǒ cóng Chester lái.**
  • Nǐ zuò shénme gōngzuò?
  • **Wǒ shì lǜshī.**

2 • Duìbuqǐ, dàxué zài nǎr?
  • **Wǒ bú shì běndìrén.**
  • Nǐ shì Jiānádàrén ma? Yīngguórén?
    Měiguórén?
  • **Wo shì Yīngguórén. Nǐ ne?**
  • Wǒ shì Yìdàlìrén.
  • **Nǐ shì xuésheng ma?**
  • Bù, wǒ jiāo Yìdàlìwén. Nǐ ne?
  • **Wǒ yě shì lǎoshī.**
  • Wǒ jiào Elena Chéng. Nǐ ne?
  • **Wǒ jiào** + your name. **Hěn**
    gāoxìng rènshi nǐ.
  • Wó yě hěn gāoxìng rènshi nǐ.

Page 22 Quiz

1 Hong Kong; 2 liù, shí; 3 sān bā wǔ jiǔ
bā; 4 your phone number; 5 de;
6 occupation; 7 gōngchéngshī/
gōngchǎng, yīyuàn/yīshēng, dàxué/
xuésheng, dǎoyóu is a tour guide;
8 Fǎguórén, Déguórén.

Unit 3

Pages 24-25 Introducing friends, colleagues and family

2 ● David, zhè shì wǒ tóngshì, Liáng Xiǎoxiá jīnglǐ.
 ◆ Hěn gāoxìng rènshi nǐ, Liáng jīnglǐ. Wǒ **jiào** David. **Zhè** shì **wǒde** míngpiàn.

 *a colleague; b manager; c **jiào** ... **Zhè** ... **wǒde** ...*

3 ● David, zhè shì wǒ **nǚ péngyou** Jiǎng Yuányuan.
 ◆ Hěn gāoxìng rènshi nǐ.
 ● Gěi nǐ jièshào wǒde **péngyou** Huáng Jiànhuán, hé Xǔ Qīng.
 ◆ **Hěn gāoxìng rènshi nǐmen.**

5 ● Wǎnshang hǎo. Zhè shì wǒ **mèimei** Jessica. Jessica, gěi nǐ jièshào wǒde péngyou, Xǔ Qīng.
 ◆ Hěn gāoxìng rènshi nǐ. Zhè shì wǒ zhàngfu, **Lǎo Dèng**.
 ● Hěn gāoxìng rènshi nǐmen.
 ◆ Wǒmen yě hěn gāoxìng rènshi nǐ.
 ● Nǐmen cóng nǎr lái?
 ◆ Wǒmen shì **Xiānggǎngrén**.
 Jessica is younger than David; Xǔ Qīng's husband is Lǎo Dèng; they're from Hong Kong.

6 Zhè shì wǒmen jiā de zhàopiàn. Zhè shì wǒ **àiren** Lǎo Dèng, nà shì wǒde **nǚ'ér** Tíngtíng. Nà shì wǒ **bàba** hé **māma**. Nà shì wǒ **nǎinai**.
 husband, daughter, mother, father, paternal grandmother.

Pages 26-27 Saying how old you are and talking about your family

2 wǔ, bāshí, shí, shísì, liùshíjiǔ, jiǔshíliù, sì
 40 not mentioned.

3 shísān, shíwǔ, sānshíjiǔ, sìshíbā, shíbā, èrshísì

5 ● Nǐ jǐ suì le?
 ◆ Wǒ **bā** suì.

● Nǐ duō dà le?
 ◆ Wǒ **èrshíwǔ** suì.
 ● Nǐ duō dà le?
 ◆ Wǒ **shíqī** suì.
 ● Nǐ duō dà suìshu le?
 ◆ Wǒ **bāshíqī** suì.
 8; 25; 17; 87.

7 ● Xiè Zhèngkǎi, nǐ jiéhūn le ma?
 ◆ Wǒ jiéhūn le, wǒ tàitai shì Běijīngrén.
 ● Nǐ yǒu háizi ma?
 ◆ Wǒ yǒu yī ge érzi.
 ● Zhōng Jiéníng, nǐ ne? Nǐ jiéhūn le ma?
 ◆ Wǒ líhūn le. Wǒ méi yǒu háizi. Nǐ ne, nǐ jiéhūn le ma?
 ● Wǒ jiéhūn le, wǒ yǒu yī ge érzi hé liǎng ge nǚ'ér.
 Zhōng Jiéníng is divorced, the other two are married.

8 *Xiè Zhèngkǎi has a son; Zhōng Jiéníng has no children; Iwan Jones has a son and 2 daughters.*

Page 28 Put it all together

1 *a 1 son; b 2 younger sisters; c 2 daughters; d 12 friends; e 1 older brother; f 2 older sisters.*

2 wǔshí; sìshísān; jiǔshíjiǔ; bāshí; yī bǎi; bāshíbā.

3 *a Jiànzhōng hé Hǎijiāo yǒu sì ge háizi; b Xiǎoqīng yǒu yī ge jiějie; c Xiǎoqīng de dìdi dānshēn; d Xiǎoqīng yǒu yī ge nǚ'ér; e Zìqiáng de àiren jiào Xiǎoqīng.*

Page 29 Now you're talking!

1 ● Nà shì nǐ zhàngfu ma?
 ◆ Shìde, nà shì wǒ(de) zhàngfu.
 ● **Zhè shì nǐ nǚ'ér ma?**
 ◆ Shìde, zhè shì wǒ(de) nǚ'ér.
 ● **Tā jǐ suì le?**
 ◆ Tā shíyī suì.
 The daughter is 11.

2 ● Nǐ jiào shénme?
 ◆ **Wǒ jiào Steve.**

- Nǐ cóng nǎr lái?
- **Wǒ cóng Exeter lái.**
- Nǐ jiéhūn le ma?
- **Wǒ jiéhūn le.**
- Nǐ tàitai jiào shénme?
- **Tā jiào Olga.**
- Nǐmen yǒu háizi ma?
- **Wǒmen yǒu liǎng ge háizi.**
- Nǐ érzi jǐ suì le?
- **Tā bā suì.**
- Nǐ nǚ'ér ne?
- **Tā liù suì.**

Page 30 Quiz

1 a younger brother; *2* 44; *3* 79 qīshíjiǔ; *4* ge; *5* liǎng, háizi; *6* nǐ duō dà le?; *7* nǚ'ér, tàitai, māma, wàipó; *8* Zhè shì Zhōng Wěi zhǔrèn.

Unit 4

Pages 32-33 Ordering tea, coffee and other drinks

2
- Nǐmen yào shénme?
- **Yī** bēi chá.
- Wǒ yào sān **bēi** kāfēi.
- Wǒmen **yào** liǎng bēi **chá**.
- Gěi nǐmen.
- Xièxie.
- **Bú xiè.**
They order two cups of tea.

3
- Xiānsheng, nǐ yào hē shénme?
- Wǒ yào **yī bēi hóng chá**, xièxie.
- Xiǎojie, nǐ yào hē shénme?
- Wǒ yào **yī bēi lǜ chá**, xièxie.
- Bú kèqi.
Lín Guóqiáng: black tea; Zhào Měilì: green tea.

5
- Nín yào shénme?
- Wǒ yào yī guàn kělè hé liǎng guàn píjiǔ.
He wants a cola and two beers.

6
- Wǒ yào sì píng píjiǔ.
- Sì píng píjiǔ, xièxie.
- Nín yào shénme?
- Wǒ yào yī bēi júzi zhī.
- Yī bēi júzi zhī, xièxie.

- Nǐmen yào hē shénme?
- Sān píng kuàngquán shuǐ.
- Sān píng kuàngquán shuǐ, xièxie.
- Yī bēi pútáojiǔ hé liǎng guàn kělè.
- Yī bēi pútáojiǔ hé liǎng guàn kělè, xièxie.
4 bottles of beer; 1 glass of orange juice; 3 bottles of mineral water; 1 glass of wine and 2 cans of cola.

7 liǎng bēi chá; yī bēi shuǐ; yī píng kuàngquán shuǐ; wǔ guàn kělè; liù píng píjiǔ; yī píng pútáojiǔ; sì bēi júzi zhī.

Page 34 Offering someone a drink

2
- Nǐ hǎo Zhāng Méi, nǐ hǎo Riley xiānsheng. Qǐng jìn, qǐng jìn.
- Lǐ Wěi, nǐ hǎo ma?
- Wǒ hěn hǎo. Qǐng zuò. Zhāng Méi, nǐ hē shénme?
- Wǒ hē lǜ chá, xièxie.
- Riley xiānsheng, nín yào hē shénme?
- Wǒ hē hóng chá. Xièxie.
- Nín yào jiā niúnǎi ma? Nín yào jiā táng ma?
- Bú yào, xièxie.
- Bú xiè.
Zhāng Méi: green tea; Jon Riley: black tea. No milk or sugar.

3
- Nǐ hǎo, Zhāng Méi, qǐng jìn.
- Xièxie, Lín xiānsheng, nín hǎo ma?
- Wǒ hěn hǎo. Qǐng zuò. Nǐ hē chá ma?
- Wǒ yào hóng chá.
- Qǐng hē chá.
- Zhè ge chá hěn hǎohē.
- Xièxie.

Page 35 Making choices

2
- Riley xiānsheng, Braun tàitai, nǐmen hǎo. Qǐng jìn, qǐng zuò.
- Xièxie, Lǐ Wěi Zhǔrèn, nǐ hǎo ma?
- Wǒ hěn hǎo. Nǐmen yào hē shénme? Riley xiānsheng, nǐ hē chá háishi kāfēi?
- Wǒ hē lǜ chá, xièxie.

- Braun tàitai, nǐ ne? Chá háishi kāfēi?
- ◆ Wǒ yào kāfēi jiā niúnǎi. Bú yào táng, xièxie.
- Hollmann xiānsheng, nǐ ne?
- ◆ Wǒ yě yīyàng, xièxie.

Offered tea or coffee. Jon: green tea; Elke and Eric: coffee with milk, no sugar.

3 ● Jon, Lisa, wǒ qǐng nǐmen hē jiǔ. Nǐmen yào hē shénme?
- ◆ Wǒ hē pútáojiǔ.
- ● Wǒ yě yīyàng.
- ◆ Bái pútáojiǔ háishi hóng pútáojiǔ?
- ● Wǒ yào hóng pútáojiǔ xièxie.
- ◆ Lisa, nǐ yào bái pútáojiǔ háishi hóng pútáojiǔ?
- ● Wǒ yào bái pútáojiǔ, xièxie.
- ◆ Wǒ yào píjiǔ. … Xiānsheng, wǒmen yào yī bēi hóng pútáojiǔ, yī bēi bái pútáojiǔ hé yī bēi píjiǔ.
- ● … Gān bēi, gān bēi.

Zhāng Méi: beer, Jon: red wine and Lisa: white wine.

4 *a* Nǐ yào lǜ chá háishi huā chá; *b* hóng pútáojiǔ háishi bái pútáojiǔ; *c* kuàngquán shuǐ háishi júzi zhī; *d* píjiǔ háishi kělè?

Page 36 Put it all together

1 *a* Bú kèqi; *b* Wǒ yào yì bēi lǜ chá; *c* Xièxie; *d* Wǒmen dōu hē chá; *e* Bú yào, xièxie.

2 *a* 3 glasses of red wine and 1 bottle of cola; *b* 2 cups of black tea, 5 cups of coffee and 1 cup of iced black tea; *c* 9 cans of orange juice, 4 bottles of mineral water; *d* 1 bottle of beer, 1 glass of white wine, 2 cans of cola.

3 *a* **yī bēi** hóng pútáojiǔ; *b* **liù guàn** píjiǔ; *c* **liǎng píng** júzi zhī; *d* **qī bēi** nǎi chá; *e* **sì bēi** kāfēi; *f* **sān píng** píjiǔ; *g* **wǔ bēi** bái pútáojiǔ; *h* **yī píng** kuàngquán shuǐ.

4 Nín yào hē shénme? Zhè ge chá hěn hǎohē.

Nǐmen yào kuàngquán shuǐ háishi júzi zhī?/Nǐmen yào júzi zhī háishi kuàngquán shuǐ?
Wǒ yào yī píng kělè.

Page 37 Now you're talking

1 ● Nǐmen hǎo. Nǐmen yào shénme?
- ◆ **Wǒmen dōu yào chá.**
- ● Nǐmen yào shénme chá? Hóng chá, lǜ chá háishi huā chá?
- ◆ **Wǒ yào yī bēi lǜ chá.**
- ● Tāmen yào shénme chá?
- ◆ **Tāmen yào yī bēi hóng chá hé yī bēi huā chá.**
- ● Hǎo de. Gěi nǐmen chá.

2 ● Nín hǎo. Qǐng jìn, qǐng zuò.
- ◆ **Xièxie.**
- ● Bú xiè. Nín hē chá háishi kāfēi?
- ◆ **Wǒ hē chá xièxie.**
- ● Nín yào lǜ chá háishi hóng chá?
- ◆ **Wǒ yào hóng chá.**
- ● Nín yào jiā niúnǎi ma? Nín yào jiā táng ma?
- ◆ **Bú yào, xièxie.**
- ● Gěi nín.
- ◆ **Zhè ge chá hěn hǎohē.**

3 ◆ **Nǐ yào píjiǔ ma? Wǒ qǐng nǐ.**
- ◆ Wǒ hē hóng pútáojiǔ.
- ● **Yī bēi hóng pútáojiǔ hé yī píng píjiǔ.**
- ◆ Gěi nǐ yī bēi hóng pútáojiǔ hé yī píng píjiǔ.
- ● **Gān bēi!**

Page 38 Quiz

1 xièxie; 2 bú xiè/bú kèqi; 3 hóng; 4 sit down; 5 píng; 6 ge; 7 háishi; 8 Bú yào niúnǎi xièxie.

Checkpoint 1
Pages 39-42

1 *a* zǎoshang hǎo; *b* hěn gāoxìng rènshi nǐ; *c* zhè ge chá hěn hǎohē; *d* wǒ hén hǎo, xièxie; *e* qǐng zuò; *f* wǒ bú yào, xièxie; *g* bú kèqi; *h* nǐ duō dà le?; *i* wǎn'ān; *j* zhè shì wǒde míngpiàn.

2 a jiǔbā; b guó; c Yīngwén;
d Àodàlìyà; e shuǐ; f wàipó;
g péngyou; h líng.

3 a Nǐ jiào shénme? b Nǐ duō dà le?
c Nǐ shì nǎ guó rén? d Nǐ zuò shénme
gōngzuò?

4 a ✗ èrshí-wǔ; b ✗ sìshí-qī; c ✓;
d ✗ jiǔshí-sì.

5 Hong Kong 00852; Japan 0081;
Indonesia 0062; Thailand 0066;
Singapore 0065; Vietnam 0084;
Malaysia 0060; Philippines 0063.

7 ● Nǐ shì nǎ guó rén?
   ◆ Wǒ shì **Yīngguórén**. Wǒ māma shì
      Zhōngguórén.
   ● Wǒ shì Běijìngrén. Nǐ lái Zhōngguó
      dùjià háishi gōngzuò?
   ◆ **Dùjià**.
   ● Nǐ jiào shénme?
   ◆ Nicola. Nǐ ne?
   ● Wǒ jiào Chén Guóqiáng.
   ◆ Nǐ duō dà le?
   ● Wǒ èrshísān suì. Nǐ ne?
   ◆ **Èrshíyī** suì. Wǒ shì **xuésheng**. Nǐ
      zuò shénme gōngzuò?
   ● Wǒ shì gōngchéngshī.
   ◆ Wǒ bàba yě shì **gōngchéngshī**
   ● Nicola, wǒ qǐng nǐ hē píjiǔ.
   ◆ Wǒ yào yī bēi júzi zhī, xièxie.
      Glass of orange juice.

8 a 13 shísān; b 15 shíwǔ; c 22 èrshí'èr;
d 30 sānshí.

9 a wǒ shì Zhōngguórén; b tā shì
Měiguórén.

10 a chá *tea*; b shuǐ *water*; c bái *white*;
d hóng *red*.

Unit 5

Pages 44-45 Asking what there is in town and whereabouts it is

3 Zhèr yǒu gōngyuán hé huāyuán. Yǒu
hěn duō shāngdiàn hé cānguǎn.
*Park, garden, many shops and
restaurants.*

4 ● Qǐng wèn, yǒu wǎngbā ma?
   ◆ Méi yǒu. Zhèr méi yǒu wǎngbā.
   ● Yǒu xīcānguǎn ma?
   ◆ Yǒu, yǒu hěn duō cānguǎn.
   ● Qǐng wèn, zhèr yǒu bówùguǎn ma?
   ◆ Yǒu.
   ● Yǒu fúzhuāng shìchǎng ma?
   ◆ Yǒu fúzhuāng shìchǎng.
   *internet café ✗; western restaurant ✓;
   museum ✓; clothes market ✓*

6 ● Shāngdiàn zài shì zhōngxīn;
      bówùguǎn zài shì zhōngxīn de běi
      biān. Zhèr yǒu gōngyuán. Cānguǎn
      zài gōngyuán pángbiān.
   ● Qǐng wèn, yǒu yínháng ma?
   ● Yǒu. Yínháng zài huāyuán duìmiàn.
   ◆ Yǒu wǎngbā ma?
   ● Méi yǒu wǎngbā.
   ◆ Xièxie.
   A restaurants; B bank; C museum.

7 ● Qǐng wèn, yǒu fúzhuāng shìchǎng
      ma?
   ◆ Fúzhuāng shìchǎng zài huǒchēzhàn
      de duìmiàn.
   Opposite the station.

Pages 46-47 Finding out how far places are and when they're open

2 ● Qǐng wèn, fùjìn yǒu méi yǒu
      yínháng?
   ◆ Yǒu, shì zhōngxīn yǒu yínháng.
   ● Yuǎn ma?
   ◆ Bù yuǎn, zǒulù wǔ fēnzhōng.
   In town centre, five minutes' walk.

3 ● Qǐng wèn, fùjìn yǒu méi yǒu chāojí
      shìchǎng?
   ◆ Fùjìn méi yǒu. Chāojí shìchǎng bú
      jìn, sān gōnglǐ yuǎn.
   ● Xièxie.
   3km away.

4 ● Qǐng wèn, yǒu yóuyǒngchí ma?
   ◆ Yǒu.
   ● Yuǎn ma?
   ◆ Bú jìn, hěn yuǎn. Yóuyǒngchí zài
      shì zhōngxīn de xī biān. Zǒulù
      sìshíwǔ fēnzhōng.

Not near, very far, 45 minutes' walk.

6 • Yóuyǒngchí **měi tiān** kāimén
   ◆ Táocí bówùguǎn **xīngqītiān**, **xīngqīyī** hé **xīngqīsì** guānmén.
   • **Xīngqīsān** yǒu zhǎnlǎnhuì.
   Swimming pool open every day; porcelain museum closed Sunday, Monday, Thursday; exhibition on Wednesday.

7 • Yóujú jīntiān zǎoshang kāimén ma?
   ◆ Yóujú měi tiān kāimén.
   • Xīngqīliù kāimén ma?
   ◆ Yóujú xīngqīliù shàngwǔ hé xiàwǔ kāimén. Xīngqīliù wǎnshang guānmén.
   • Xīngqītiān kāimén ma?
   ◆ Xīngqītiān zǎoshang hé wǎnshang guānmén.

   1 xīngqīliù xiàwǔ; xīngqīliù shàngwǔ kāimén.

   2 xīngqīliù wǎnshang; xīngqītiān zǎoshang; xīngqītiān wǎnshang guānmén.

Page 48 Put it all together

1 *a the park isn't far; b there's no internet café; c the museum is opposite the bank; d there's no supermarket nearby; e twenty-five minutes' walk; f there are lots of shops; g the bank is next to the market.*

2 *a Sunday; b Monday to Saturday 8am to 5pm; Sunday 9am to 4pm; c 2pm and 6:30pm; d no, open only Friday to Saturday.*

Page 49 Now you're talking

1 • **Qǐng wèn, yǒu gōngyuán ma?**
   ◆ Yǒu. Hěn jìn – wǔ bǎi mǐ.
   • **Zhèr yǒu shāngdiàn ma?**
   ◆ Yǒu hěn duō shāngdiàn; zài shì zhōngxīn.
   • **Xièxie. Zàijiàn.**

2 • **Fùjìn yǒu méi yǒu wǎngbā?**
   ◆ Méi yǒu. Wǎngbā zài shì zhōngxīn de běi biān. Yuǎn, hěn yuǎn, wǔ gōnglǐ.
   • **Yóujú lí zhèr yuǎn ma?**
   ◆ Yóujú bù yuǎn. Zài shì zhōngxīn, zài yínháng pángbiān.
   • **Yóujú bù yuǎn. Zài shì zhōngxīn, zài yínháng pángbiān. Xièxie.**
   ◆ Bú kèqi.
   • **Yínháng jīntiān kāimén ma?**
   ◆ Jīntiān yínháng guānmén.
   • **Míngtiān kāimén ma?**
   ◆ Shìde. Míngtiān kāimén.

Page 50 Quiz

1 qǐng wèn; 2 yóuyǒngchí swimming pool; 3 xiàwǔ; 4 next to; 5 Yǒu méi yǒu xīcānguǎn? 6 méi yǒu, guānmén, jìn; 7 Yes, banks open every day in China; 8 hěnduō.

Unit 6
Pages 52–53 Asking the way and following directions

2 • Qǐng wèn, zuìjìn de cèsuǒ zài nǎr?
   ◆ Cèsuǒ zài **lóushàng**, zài **sān céng**.
   • Xièxie.
   Toilets upstairs, 2nd floor (UK).

3 • Qǐng wèn, cèsuǒ zài nǎr?
   ◆ Duìbuqǐ, **wǒ bù zhīdao**.
   • Zuìjìn de cèsuǒ zài **lóuxià**, zài **sān céng**.
   ◆ Duìbuqǐ, wǒ bù dǒng. Cèsuǒ zài lóuxià ma?
   • Lóuxià.
   a wǒ bù zhīdao – she doesn't know; b downstairs, 2nd floor (UK).

4 • Qǐng wèn, cèsuǒ **zài nǎr?**
   ◆ Cèsuǒ zài nǐde **zuǒ** biān. Jiù **zài** nàbiān.
   On the left.

6 • Qǐng wèn, qù huǒchēzhàn zěnme zǒu?

- ◆ **Yìzhí zǒu, dào lùkǒu, wǎng zuǒ guǎi.**
  Straight on as far as the crossroads, turn left.

7 ● Qǐng wèn, qù Xuéyuàn Lù zěnme zǒu?
  - ◆ Xuéyuàn Lù ... wǎng **běi** zǒu dào **hónglǜdēng**. Wǎng **yòu** guǎi, Xuéyuàn Lù zài nǐde **zuǒ** biān.

8 ● Duìbuqǐ, wǒ mí lù le. Qǐng wèn, qù Xuéyuàn Lù zěnme zǒu?
  - ◆ Xuéyuàn Lù bù yuǎn. Wǎng běi zǒu. Zǒu dào dì yī ge lùkǒu, wǎng yòu guǎi. Yìzhí zǒu dào dì èr ge hónglǜdēng. Xuéyuàn Lù zài nǐde zuǒ biān.
  - ● Wǒ wǎng běi zǒu dào lùkǒu, wǎng yòu guǎi, yìzhí zǒu dào dì èr ge hónglǜdēng. Xuéyuàn Lù zài wǒde zuǒ biān.
  - ◆ Duì. Xuéyuàn Lù zài nǐde zuǒ biān.
  - ● Xièxie.
  A = Xueyuan Road.

Pages 54-55 Talking about where people live and getting hep to understand

2 ● George, nǐ zhù zài nǎr?
  - ◆ Wǒ zhù zài jiāoqū.
  - ● Nǐ ne, Jacquie? Nǐ zhù zài nǎr?
  - ◆ Wǒ zhù zài nóngcūn.
  - ● Fran, nǐ zhù zài nǎr?
  - ◆ Wǒ yě zhù zài nóngcūn.
  - ● Thomas, Lizzie, nǐmen zhù zài nǎr? Nǐmen zhù zài shì zhōngxīn ma?
  - ◆ Wǒmen zhù zài hǎi biān.
  George: suburbs; Jacquie: country; Fran: country; Thomas & Lizzie: by the sea.

3 ● Fēng Yìmín, nǐ ne? Nǐ zhù zài nǎr?
  - ◆ Wǒ zhù zài Shànghǎi, zài hǎi biān. Wǒ jiějie yě zhù zài Shànghǎi, dànshì wǒ bàba hé māma zhù zài jiāoqū.
  - ● Nǐde yéye hé nǎinai zhù zài Shànghǎi ma?

- ◆ Tāmen bú zhù zài Shànghǎi shì. Tāmen zhù zài nóngcūn, zài Shànghǎi běi biān
  Fēng Yìmín: Shanghai, by the sea. Her sister: Shanghai. Her parents: in the suburbs. Her grandparents: in the country, north of Shanghai.

5 ● Zhè shì wǒ péngyou Měilì.
  - ◆ Hěn gāoxìng rènshi nǐmen. Wǒ yě shì Shànghǎirén.
  - ● Qǐng zài shuō yíbiàn.
  - ◆ Wǒ shì Shànghǎirén – wǒ cóng Shànghǎi lái. Wǒ zhù zài gōngyù, hǎi biān. Wǒde gōngyù zài èrshísān céng.
  - ● Měilì, qǐng shuō màn yìdiǎn.
  - ◆ Wǒde gōngyù zài èrshísān céng.
  a in Shanghai, by the sea; b 22nd floor (UK).

6 ● Wǒ shēng zài Sūzhōu, xiànzài zhù zài Shànghǎi.
  - ● Qǐng zài shuō yíbiàn.
  - ● Wǒ zhù zài Shànghǎi, dànshì wǒ shēng zài Sūzhōu.
  - ◆ Duìbuqǐ, Měilì, wǒ bù dǒng. Nǐ huì shuō Yīngyǔ ma?
  - ● Huì shuō yìdiǎn. I was born in Sūzhōu but now – xiànzài – I live in Shànghǎi.
  - ● Nǐde Yīngyǔ hěn hǎo!
  - ● Nǎli, nǎli.

Page 56 Put it all together

1 *a* Qǐng zài shuō yìbiàn; *b* Nǐ zhù zài Déguó ma?; *c* Wǒ bù zhīdao; *d* Wǒ shuō yìdiǎn Zhōngwén; *e* Qǐng shuō màn yìdiǎn; *f* Nǐ shuō Déwén ma?; *g* Wǒ bù dǒng.
  Wǎng dōng guǎi *Turn towards the east.*

2 *a* shuō; *b* zài; *c* zhù; *d* zǒu; *e* zhīdao; *f* huì.

3 c; h; g; e or f; a; f or e; d; b.

Page 57 Now you're talking

1 ● Duìbuqǐ, zuìjìn de cèsuǒ zài nǎr?
  ◆ Cèsuǒ zài lóushàng, wǔ céng.
  ● Qǐng zài shuō yībiàn.
  ◆ Cèsuǒ zài lóushàng, wǔ céng.
  ● Xièxie.
  She said the toilets are upstairs on the fourth floor (UK).

2 ● Qǐng wèn, nǐ huì shuō Yīngyǔ ma?
  ◆ Duìbuqǐ. Bú huì.
  ● Qǐng wèn, qù Zhōngshān Fàndiàn zěnme zǒu?
  ◆ Wǎng dōng zǒu, dào dì èr ge hónglǜdēng, wǎng yòu guǎi.
  ● Duìbuqǐ, wǒ bù dǒng.
  ◆ Wǎng dōng zǒu, dào dì èr ge hónglǜdēng, wǎng yòu guǎi, yìzhí zǒu, jiù shì Zhōngshān Fàndiàn.
  ● Yuǎn ma?
  ◆ Bù yuǎn, zǒulù shíwǔ fēnzhōng.

3 ● Nǐ zhù zài nǎr?
  ◆ Wǒ zhù zài Xiānggǎng.
  ● Nǐde bàba hé māma yě zhù zài Xiānggǎng ma?
  ◆ Bù, tāmen zhù zài Shànghǎi. Wǒmen quán jiā dōu zhù zài nàr.
  ● Duìbuqǐ, wǒ bù dǒng quán jiā
  ◆ Quán jiā – bàba hé māma, jiějie, yéye hé nǎinai, wàigōng, wàipó …
  ● Wǒ dǒng le.
  ◆ Nǐ Zhōngwén shuō de hěn hǎo!
  ● Nǎli, nǎli.

Page 58 Quiz

1 Eastern capital; *2* women's; *3* Where's the cashpoint?, Where's the nearest cashpoint?; *4* left; *5* nǎli nǎli; *6* yǒu; *7* 10th floor; *8* Wǒ zài Běijīng gōngzuò. Nǐ zài Xiānggǎng gōngzuò ma?

Unit 7

Page 60 Understanding prices in renminbi

1 yī yuán
  yī jiǎo
  yī fēn
  shí yuán
  shí yuán sān jiǎo
  shí yuán sān jiǎo sì fēn
  wǔshí yuán
  bāshíwǔ yuán qī jiǎo wǔ fēn

2 *a* bā yuán
  b bā jiǎo qī fēn
  c shíjiǔ yuán wǔ jiǎo
  d sìshí'èr yuán
  e liùshísì yuán wǔ jiǎo wǔ fēn
  f jiǔshí yuán jiǔ jiǎo jiǔ fēn

4 ● Bōluó duōshao qián?
  ◆ Sì yuán wǔ jiǎo.
  ● Xiāngjiāo duōshao qián?
  ◆ Sān yuán qián yī jīn.
  ● Mángguǒ duōshao qián?
  ◆ Liù yuán.
  ● Píngguǒ ne?
  ◆ Liǎng yuán qián yī jīn.
  ● Lìzhī duōshao qián?
  ◆ Shí yuán wǔ jiǎo qián yī jīn.
  ● Wǒ mǎi yī jīn.
  pineapple ¥4.50, bananas ¥3, mango ¥6, apples ¥2, lychees ¥10.50.

Page 61 Asking for what you want

3 ● Nín hǎo. Nín mǎi shénme?
  ◆ Wǒ yào mǎi míngxìnpiàn
  ● Yào duōshao?
  ◆ Wǒ mǎi zhè ge, nà ge, wǔ ge zhè ge. Duōshao qián?
  ● Shísì yuán.
  Postcards, cost ¥14 for 7 (this one, that one, 5 of those).

4 ● Hái yào biéde ma?
  ◆ Wǒ mǎi zhè ge màozi. Duōshao qián?
  ● Shí yuán.
  ◆ Wǒ yào fángshàiyóu.

- Fángshàiyóu èrshísān yuán wǔ jiǎo.
- **Yǒu lǚyóu dìtú ma?**
- Duìbuqǐ, méi yǒu. Hái yào biéde ma?
- Bú yào le, xièxie. **Qiǎokèlì duōshao qián?**
- Liù yuán.
- Wǒ mǎi yī bāo qiǎokèlì. Yīgòng duōshao qián?
- **Yīgòng, wǔshísān yuán wǔ jiǎo.**
- Xièxie.
- Zàijiàn.

She spent ¥53.50 altogether.

Page 62 Shopping in a department store

2
- Nín xiǎng mǎi shénme?
- Wǒ zài zhǎo lǐngdài.
- Hǎo de. Zhè shì zhēnsī lǐngdài.
- Yǒu qítā yánsè ma?
- Wǒmen yǒu lánsè, hóngsè, lǜsè, huángsè.
- Wó mǎi lánsè de lǐngdài. Wǒ zài zhǎo yángróng pījiān wéijīn.
- Hǎo de. Wǒmen yǒu hēisè, hóngsè, báisè, lánsè, huángsè, lǜsè.
- Hēisè. Wó mǎi hēisè pījiān. Duōshao qián?
- Yī bǎi sānshí'èr yuán.

Blue tie; black pashmina.

3
- Nín xiǎng mǎi shénme?
- Wǒ zài zhǎo chènshān. Báisè chènshān. Wǒ xiǎng kànkan nà jiàn.
- Nín yào duō dà de?
- Zhōng hào. Wǒ kěyǐ shìshi ma?
- Kěyǐ.
- Tài xiǎo le. Yǒu dà hào ma?

a false, he wants a white shirt; b true; c true.

Page 63 Bargaining

2
- Zhè ge Zhōngwén jiào shénme?
- Shānshuǐ huà.
- Zhè ge **hěn piàoliang.** Duōshao qián?
- Yī qiān yuán.

- Yǒu xiǎo de ma?
- Duìbuqǐ, méi yǒu.
- **Piányi yìdiǎn ba?**
- Zhè ge **hěn piàoliang.** Jiǔ bǎi wǔ shí yuán.
- **Tài guì le.** Jiǔ bǎi **yuán, zěnmeyàng?**
- **Hǎo ba.**

Final price ¥900.

3
- Nǐ hǎo. Nǐ mǎi shénme?
- Nà ge zhēnzhū ěrhuán duōshao qián?
- Sān bǎi bāshí yuán.
- Tài guì le! Xiǎo zhēnzhū. Piányi yìdiǎn ba?
- Hěn piàoliang de zhēnzhū. Bú guì.
- Tài guì le. Yī bǎi yuán?
- Èr bǎi wǔshí yuán.
- Yī bǎi wǔshí yuán.
- Èr bǎi yuán, zěnmeyàng?
- Hǎo ba. Èr bǎi yuán.

a ¥380; b ¥200.

Page 64 Put it all together

1 ¥21.77: èrshíyī yuán qī jiǎo qī fēn

2 a **guì** *expensive*, the rest are colours; b **qiǎokèlì** *chocolate*, the rest are fruit; c **zhēnsī** *silk*, the rest are shops; d **piàoliang** *beautiful*, the rest are sizes; e **míngxìnpiàn** *postcards*, the rest are clothing.

3 a Nín xiǎng **mǎi** shénme?
b Wǒ zài **zhǎo** chènshān.
c **Zhè** shì zhēnsī chènshān.
d **Yǒu** qítā yánsè **ma?**
e **Wǒmen** yǒu báisè, lánsè, huángsè, **lǜsè** …
f Wǒ mǎi lánsè de chènshān. Wǒ kěyǐ **shìshi** ma?

4
- Nín mǎi shénme?
- Wǒ yào mǎi fēngzheng.
- Zhè ge hěn piàoliang.
- Duōshao qián?
- Èr bǎi wǔshí yuán.
- Tài guì le! Piányi yìdiǎn ba?
- Èr bǎi yuán, zěnmeyàng?

◆ Hǎo ba.
a kite; 200 yuan.

Page 65 Now you're talking

1 ● Nǐ hǎo. Nǐ mǎi shénme?
◆ **Xiāngjiāo duōshao qián?**
● Sān kuài yī jīn.
◆ **Wǒ mǎi yī jīn xiāngjiāo**
● Hái yào biéde ma?
◆ **Wǒ mǎi liǎng ge nà ge.**
● Qiǎokèlì duōshao qián?
◆ Bā yuán wǔ jiǎo.
● **Qǐng zài shuō yíbiàn.**
◆ Bā yuán wǔ jiǎo.

2 ● Nín mǎi shénme?
◆ **Wǒ zài zhǎo zhēnsī lǐngdài.**
Wǒ xiǎng kànkan zhè ge.
● Hěn piàoliang de lǐngdài.
◆ **Yǒu qítā yánsè ma?**
● Wǒmen yǒu lánsè, hóngsè, lǜsè, huángsè.

3 ● Hěn piàoliang de xiàngliàn. Dà zhēnzhū … liǎng qiān liù bǎi yuán.
◆ **That is 2,600 yuan.**
Tài guì le.
● Bú guì!
◆ **Piányi yìdiǎn ba?**
Yī qiān liǎng bǎi yuán zěnmeyàng?
● Hǎo ba.
◆ **Xièxie. Zàijiàn.**

Page 66 Quiz

1 10, 2; *2* Do you want anything else?; *3* zhù *live*, shuō *speak*; *4* wǔ ge nà ge; *5* XXL; *6* bú shì, bú yào, méi yǒu; *7* Wǒ zài zhǎo chúnmáo shàngyī; *8* Tài hòu le.

Checkpoint 2
Pages 67–70

1 ● Qǐng wèn, fùjìn yǒu méi yǒu **yínháng?**
◆ Yǒu. Yìzhí zǒu dào dì yī ge hónglǜdēng, wǎng zuǒ guǎi …
● Duìbuqǐ, qǐng shuō màn yīdiǎn. Wǒ bù dǒng.

◆ Yìzhí zǒu dào hónglǜdēng, wǎng zuǒ guǎi. Yínháng zài Shànghǎi Lù, zài nǐde yòu biān.

● Qǐng wèn, **huǒchēzhàn** zài nǎr?
◆ Duìbuqǐ, wǒ bù zhīdao. Wǒ bú shì běndìrén.
● Qǐng wèn, huǒchēzhàn zài nǎr?
◆ Zǒu dào hónglǜdēng, wǎng yòu guǎi. Yìzhí zǒu, dào lùkǒu, wǎng zuǒ guǎi dào Xuéyuàn Lù. Yìzhí zǒu, huǒchēzhàn jiù zài nàbiān.
● Yuǎn ma?
◆ Bù yuǎn, hěn jìn, wǔ bǎi mǐ. Zǒulù wǔ fēnzhōng.
● Qǐng wèn, fùjìn yǒu **chāojí shìchǎng** ma?
◆ Chāojí shìchǎng zài shì zhōngxīn. Yìzhí zǒu dào hónglǜdēng, wǎng zǒu guǎi. Wǎng yòu guǎi dào Dōng Fāng Lù. Nàr yǒu yī jiā chāojí shìchǎng, zài nǐde yòu biān. Zài yóujú pángbiān.

a yínháng bank E; *b* huǒchēzhàn station A; *c* chāojí shìchǎng supermarket C.

2 *a* false: Yǒu liǎng jiā jiǔbā; *b* true; *c* false: Bówùguǎn zài yínháng duìmiàn.

3 yī bēi kǎbùqínuò: shíwǔ yuán ¥15
liǎng ge hànbǎo bāo: sānshí yuán ¥30
yī ge bǐsà bǐng: shísì yuán, wǔ jiǎ ¥14.50
yī píng xiāngbīn: jiǔshíqī yuán ¥97
yī píng bāilándì: bāshíqī yuán ¥87
sān bēi wēishìjì liùshíjiǔ yuán ¥69

4 xīngqīyī; xīngqī'èr; xīngqīsān; xīngqīsì; xīngqīwǔ; xīngqīliù; xīngqītiān

5 *a* 14; *b* 90; *c* 55; *d* 73; *e* 62; *f* 十; *g* 二十二; *h* 八十; *i* 十六

6 *a* zhǎlǎnhuì; *b* fàndiàn; *c* bǎihuò shāngdiàn; *d* jiǔbā; *e* shuǐguǒdiàn.

7 *a* Kěyǐ shìshi ma?; *b* Nǐ huì shuō Yīngyǔ ma?; *c* Yǒu dà hào ma?; *d* Tài guì le, piányi yìdiǎn ba; *e* Wǒ xiǎng kànkan zhè ge; *f* Qǐng

shuō màn yìdiǎn; g Qǐng zài shuō
yībiàn; h Duìbuqǐ.

8 dōng, nán, běi
dà, xiǎo, guì
shìchǎng, chāojí shìchǎng,
shāngdiàn
chènshān, màozi, lǐngdài
xīcānguǎn, jiǔbā, cānguǎn
nóngcūn, hǎi biān, jiāoqū
xiāngjiāo, píngguǒ, lìzhī

9 a yēzi *coconut*; b yīngtáo *cherry*; c xī
guā *watermelon*; d níngméng *lemon*.

10 a *shop*; b *book*; c *flower*; d *bread*;
e *shoe*; f *stationery*.

Unit 8

Pages 72-73 Finding a hotel room and saying how long you want to stay

2 ● Nǐ hǎo. Yǒu kòng fángjiān ma?
◆ Dānrén fángjiān háishi shuāngrén
fángjiān?
● Shuāngrén fángjiān dài yùshì.
◆ Huānyíng guānglín.
● Wǎnshang hǎo. Yǒu fángjiān ma?
◆ Yǒu.
● Wǒ yào dānrén jiān dài yùshì hé
kōngtiáo.
◆ Nǐ hǎo. Wǒ yào shuāngrén jiān dài
kōngtiáo.
● Duìbuqǐ, méi yǒu kōngtiáo.
◆ Huānyíng guānglín. Wǎnshang
hǎo.
● Wǒmen yào liǎngrén fángjiān dài
yùshì hé kōngtiáo.
◆ Hǎo ba.
1 double room with en suite;
2 single room with en suite and air
conditioning; 3 double room with air
conditioning; 4 twin room with en
suite and air conditioning.

3 ● Bāo zǎocān ma?
◆ Bāo. Cānguǎn zài sì céng.
a Bāo, Bù bāo; b The restaurant's on
the 3rd floor.

5 ● Nín zhù jǐ tiān?
◆ Wǒ zhù **yī ge xīngqī.**
● Nǐmen yào zhù jǐ tiān?
◆ **Cóng jīntiān dào xīngqīsān.**
● Nín zhù jǐ wǎn?
◆ Wǒ zhù **liǎng ge wǎnshang.**

6 ● Wèi, nǐ hǎo, shì Mín Háng Fàndiàn.
◆ Yǒu kòng fángjiān ma?
● Nǐ shénme shíhou zhù?
◆ **Shíyīyuè liù hào.**
● Wèi. Shì Mín Háng Fàndiàn.
◆ Nǐ hǎo. Wǒ yào shuāngrén fángjiān
dài yùshì. **Liùyuè shísì hào**
xīngqīliù.
● Qǐng shāo děng ... Duìbuqǐ,
wǒmen zhù mǎn le.
◆ Wèi.
◆ Yǒu kòng fángjiān ma?
◆ Nǐ shénme shíhou zhù?
● **Cóng jīntiān dào wǔyuè èrshíwǔ**
hào.
◆ Qǐng shāo děng.
a 6th November; b on Saturday, 14th
June (not available); c from today until
25th May.

Page 74 Checking in

2 ● Nǐ hǎo. Wǒ yùdìng le fángjiān.
◆ Nín guì xìng?
● Wǒ xìng Qín. Wǒ yùdìng le
shuāngrén fángjiān, zhù sì ge
wǎnshang.
◆ Qǐng tián zhè zhāng biǎo .... Gěi
nín yàoshi. Fángjiān hàomǎ shì liù
qī líng.
a Qín; b double room; c 4 nights; d fill
in a form; e 670.

3 ● Wǒ yùdìng le yī ge wǎnshang
shuāngrén jiān.
◆ Nín guì xìng?
● Wǒ xìng Lǐ, jiào Lǐ Ěr.
◆ Nín hǎo, Lǐ xiānsheng. Qǐng gěi wǒ
nínde hùzhào.
● Gěi nǐ.
◆ Xièxie. Fángjiān hàomǎ shì yī èr bā
jiǔ.

- Huānyíng guānglín. Nín yùdìng
  fángjiān le ma?
- Wǒ yùdìng le yī ge xīngqī dānrén
  jiān. Wǒ xìng Zhāng.
- Nín hǎo, Zhāng xiǎojie. Qǐng tián
  zhè zhāng biǎo.
- Wǒde fángjiān hàomǎ shì
  duōshao?
- Yī jiǔ líng sān. Zhè shì nínde yàoshi.
- Xièxie.
- Huānyíng guānglín. Nín guì xìng?
- Wǒ xìng Gāo. Wǒ yùdìng le sān ge
  wǎnshang shuāngrén jiān.
- Nín hǎo, Gāo tàitai. Zhè shì nínde
  yàoshi. Nínde fángjiān hàomǎ shì
  èr liù qī bā.
- Yǒu diàntī ma?
- Yǒu, zài zuǒbiān. Qǐng gēn wǒ lái.

*Lǐ xiānsheng: double room for 1 night,
room no. 1289; Zhāng xiǎojie: single
room for 1 week, room no. 1903; Gāo
tàitai: double room for 3 nights, room
no, No.2678.*

4 *The lifts are on the left.*

Page 75 Making requests

2 • Xiǎojie. Qǐng wèn, wǒ néng yòng
  xìnyòngkǎ fù ma?
- Néng.
- Nǐ néng bù néng liù diǎn jiào xǐng
  wǒ?
- Dāngrán kěyǐ.

*He wants a) to pay by credit card, b) a
wake-up call at 6.*

3 • Xiǎojie, wǒ kěyǐ **bǎ wǒde xínglǐ liú
  zài zhèr** ma?
- Kěyǐ.
- Xiǎojie, nǐ néng bù néng **gěi wǒ
  jiào yī liàng chūzūchē**?
- Dāngrán kěyǐ.
- Wǒ néng **yòng hùliánwǎng jiēkǒu**
  ma?
- Duìbuqǐ …
- Wǒ néng **yòng zhè ge diànhuà**
  ma?
- Dāngrán kěyǐ.
- Xiǎojie, qǐng wèn. Duōshao qián?

- Èr bǎi wǔshí yuán.
- Wǒ néng **yòng xìnyòngkǎ fù** ma?
- Néng.

Page 76 Put it all together

1 *a* wǒ yào; *b* nǐ néng bù néng;
  c wǒmen zhù; *d* wǒ kěyǐ … ma; *e* gěi
  nǐ; *f* qǐng; *g* wǒmen néng … ma.

2 *a* Yǒu kòng **dānrén jiān** ma?; *b* Wǒ
  yào **shuāngrén jiān dài yùshì**;
  c Wǒ néng **yòng jiànshēnfáng** ma?;
  d Nǐ néng bù néng gěi wǒ jiào yī liàng
  chūzūchē?; *e* Qǐng gěi wǒ **yàoshi**.

3 *a* shí'èryuè èrshíwǔ hào; *b* shí'èryuè
  sānshíyī hào; *c* yīyuè yī hào; *d* èryuè
  shísì hào.

Page 77 Now you're talking

1 • Huānyíng guānglín. Wǒ néng
  bāngzhù nǐ ma?
- **Yǒu kòng fángjiān ma?**
- Shuāngrén jiān háishi liǎngrén jiān?
- **Liǎngrén jiān, dài yùshì.**
- Nǐ yào zhù jǐ wǎn?
- **Zhǐ yào jīnwǎn.**
- Yǒu kòng fángjiān.
- **Fángjiān duōshao qián?**
- Liù bǎi yuán.
- **Bāo zǎocān ma?**
- Bāo zǎocān.

2 • **Wǒ yùdìng le fángjiān.**
- Nín guì xìng?
- **Wǒ xìng Marshall.**
- Dānrén jiān dài kōngtiáo. Sān ge
  wǎnshang.
- **Wǒ zhù yí ge xīngqī.**
- Qǐng shāo děng. Hǎo, yī ge xīngqī.
  Dào sānyuè liù hào. Qǐng gěi wǒ
  nínde hùzhào.
- **Gěi nǐ hùzhào. Wǒ kěyǐ yòng
  xìnyòngkǎ fù** ma?
- Dāngrán kěyǐ.

Page 78 Quiz

1 passport; 2 Měiguórén *American*;
3 Bāo zǎocān ma?; 4 qīyuè *July*,
jiǔyuè *September*; 5 taxi; 6 Nǐ néng

bù néng qī diǎn jiào xǐng wǒ?; 7 Tā
zhù liǎng ge xīngqī; 8 a Yǒu xǐyīfáng
ma?, b Wǒ néng yòng xǐyīfáng ma?

Unit 9

Page 80 Saying where you're going

2 ● Nǐ hǎo. Wǒ néng bāngzhù nǐ ma?
  ◆ Wǒ yào qù Tiān'ānmén.
  ● Nǐ shénme shíhou qù?
  ◆ **Xiànzài.**
  ● Nǐ kěyǐ zuò **gōnggòng qìchē**
    huòzhě **chūzūchē.**
  Bus, taxi; he wants to go now.

3 ● Wǒ yào **qù** shì zhōngxīn.
  ◆ Nǐ **shénme shíhou** qù? Jīntiān
    háishi míngtiān?
  ● Míngtiān.
  ● Nǐ kěyǐ zuò dìtiě **huòzhě** chūzūchē.
  ● Hǎo. Nǐ **yǒu** dìtú ma?
  ● Gěi nǐ.
  ● Xièxie.
  ◆ Bú xiè.

Page 81 Asking about public transport

2 ● Duìbuqǐ. Wǒ yào qù Chángchéng.
    Yǒu gōnggòng qìchē ma?
  ◆ Yǒu. Zuò jiǔ yāo bā lù chē.
  ● Duō jiǔ néng dào?
  ◆ Yī ge xiǎoshí.
  ● Duìbuqǐ. Zuò jǐ lù chē qù Běihǎi
    Gōngyuán?
  ◆ Sān èr liù.
  ● Qǐng wèn, yǒu qù Tiān'ānmén de
    gōnggòng qìchē ma?
  ◆ Méi yǒu. Tiān'ānmén bù yuǎn, bù
    yuǎn.
  ● Duō jiǔ néng dào?
  ◆ Zǒulù shí fēnzhōng.
  ● Xièxie.
  ◆ Zhè ge chē qù Yōnghégōng ma?
  ● Qù.
  ◆ Chē shénme shíhou kāi?
  ● Shí fēnzhōng yǐhòu.
  ◆ Duìbuqǐ. Zhè lù chē qù Yíhéyuán
    ma?

  ● Bú qù, nín zuò sānshíwǔ lù chē. Wǔ
    fēnzhōng néng dào.
  ◆ Shénme shíhou yǒu chē qù
    Gùgōng?
  ● Měi shíwǔ fēnzhōng.
  ◆ Duō jiǔ néng dào?
  ● Wǔ fēnzhōng. Hěn jìn.
  *Beihai Park: bus no. 326; Forbidden
  City: bus every 15 minutes, takes
  5 minutes; Lama Temple every 10
  minutes; Tiananmen Square: no bus, 10
  minutes' walk; The Great Wall: bus no.
  918, takes 1 hour; Summer Palace: bus
  no. 35, takes 5 minutes to arrive.*

Page 82-83 Finding out train times and buying tickets

2 ● Duìbuqǐ, xià yī bān qù Chángzhōu
    de huǒchē jǐ diǎn kāi?
  ◆ Bā diǎn wǔshí.
  ● Duìbuqǐ, xià yī bān qù Nánjīng de
    huǒchē jǐ diǎn kāi?
  ◆ Liǎng diǎn sānshí'èr.
  ◆ Xià yī tàng qù Shànghǎi de huǒchē
    jǐ diǎn kāi?
  ◆ Wǎnshang jiǔ diǎn sānshíliù.
  ◆ Wǒ yào qù Shěnyáng. Zǎoshang
    yǒu huǒchē ma?
  ◆ Yǒu. Liù diǎn sìshíjiǔ kāi.
  ◆ Qù Qínhuángdǎo de huǒchē jǐ diǎn
    kāi?
  ◆ Shíyī diǎn èrshísān.
  *Changzou 8.50; Nanjing 2.32;
  Shanghai 9.36pm; Shenyang 6.49am;
  Qinhuangdao 11.23.*

3 ● Duìbuqǐ, xià yī bān qù Xī'ān de
    huǒchē jǐ diǎn kāi?
  ◆ Shíwǔ fēnzhōng hòu. Qī diǎn líng
    sān.
  ● Huǒchē jǐ diǎn dào Xī'ān?
  ◆ Zǎoshang liù diǎn sìshísì fēn.
  *3 a false – it leaves in 15 minutes;
  b true; c false – it arrives at 6.44pm.*

5 ● Wǒmen qù Sūzhōu.
  ◆ Nǐmen yào mǎi jǐ zhāng?
  ◆ Sì zhāng piào.
  ◆ Dānchéng háishi wǎngfǎn?
  ● Wǎngfǎn.
  ◆ Nǐmen yào yìngzuò háishi
    ruǎnzuò?
  ● Ruǎnzuò duōshao qián?
  ◆ Ruǎnzuò èrshíbā yuán, yìngzuò shí
    yuàn.
  ● Wǒ mǎi sì zhāng ruǎnzuò piào.
    Lam xiǎojie mǎi **sì** zhāng **wǎngfǎn**
    piào. Tā yào ruǎnzuò piào.

6 ● Wǎnshang hǎo. Wǒ yào qù Běijīng.
    Xià yī tàng huǒchē jǐ diǎn kāi?
  ◆ Qī diǎn bàn. Z-shísān cì chē.
  ● Huǒchē jǐ diǎn dào Běijīng?
  ◆ Zǎoshang qī diǎn líng liù.
  ● Hǎo de. Yǒu piào ma?
  ◆ Yǒu. Jǐ zhāng piào?
  ● Yī zhāng piào.
  ◆ Dānchéng háishi wǎngfǎn?
  ● Dānchéng.
  ◆ Nín yào ruǎnzuò háishi ruǎnwò?
  ● Ruǎnzuò.
  ◆ Sān bǎi qīshí'èr yuán.
  ● Wǒ kěyǐ yòng xìnyòngkǎ fù ma?
  ◆ Dāngrán kěyǐ.
  Destination: Beijing; Departure 7.30,
  arrival 7.06 am; single ticket; soft seat;
  372 yuan.

Page 84 Put it all together

1 *a* 4; *b* 3; *c* 1; *d* 2; *e* 6; *f* 5.

2 *a* zǎoshang qī diǎn bàn; *b* wǎnshang
  liù diǎn èrshísān; *c* zhōngwǔ shí'èr
  diǎn yī kè; *d* shàngwǔ shí diǎn sìshí;
  e xiàwǔ sì diǎn líng wǔ; *f* zǎoshang wǔ
  diǎn chà yī kè.

3 *a* **zǎocān** *breakfast*, the rest are parts
  of the day; *b* **zìxíngchē** *bicycle*, the
  rest are trains; *c* **píngguǒ** *apple*,
  the rest relate to time; *d* **hùzhào**
  passport, the rest are train seating;
  e **piào** *ticket*, the rest relate to telling
  the time.

4 *a* **Yǒu qù Chángchéng de gōnggòng
  qìchē ma?** Is there a bus to the
  Great Wall?
  b **Nǐ shénme shíhou qù Běijīng?**
  When are you going to Beijing?
  c **Xià yī tàng qù Nánjīng de huǒchē
  jǐ diǎn kāi?** What time is the next
  train to Nanjing?

Page 85 Now you're talking

1 ● **Yǒu qù Yíhéyuán de gōnggòng
    qìchē ma?**
  ◆ **Yǒu. Qīshíbā lù chē. Měi shí
    fēnzhōng yī tàng.**
  Bus no. 78, every 10 minutes.

  ● **Duō jiǔ néng dào?**
  ◆ **Èrshíwǔ fēnzhōng.**
  ● **Piào duōshao qián?**
  ◆ **Shíliù yuán.**
  ● **Wǒ mǎi liǎng zhāng (piào).**
  ◆ **Gěi nǐ.**
  ● **Xièxie.**
  ◆ **Bú xiè.**

2 ● **Xià yī tàng qù Xī'ān de huǒchē jǐ
    diǎn kāi?**
  ◆ **Liù diǎn sìshíwǔ fēn.**
  ● **Huǒchē jǐ diǎn dào Xī'ān?**
  ◆ **Zǎoshang qī diǎn líng wǔ.**
  ● **Wǒ yào yī zhāng piào.**
  ◆ **Dānchéng háishi wǎngfǎn?**
  ● **Dānchéng.**
  ◆ **Nǐ yào ruǎnzuò piào ma?**
  ● **Wǒ yào ruǎnwò. Duōshao qián?**
  ◆ **Liùshí'èr yuán. Gěi nǐ. Yí lù píng ān.**

Page 86 Quiz

1 8.45, jiǔ diǎn sānshí (fēn), jiǔ
diǎn bàn; *2* a bus; *3* to buy tickets;
4 háishi; *5* express, T; *6* ruǎnwò,
standing; *7* every half hour/in half
an hour's time; *8* Yínháng jǐ diǎn
guānmén?.

Unit 10

Page 88 Choosing a place to eat

2 ● Wǒmen wǎnshang chī shénme?
  ◆ Wǒ xǐhuan chuāncài.
  ● Wǒ yě xǐhuan chuāncài.
  ◆ Wǒ bù xǐhuan chuāncài - hěn là.
    Wǒmen chī jiǎozi, hǎo bù hǎo?
  ● Wǒ bù xǐhuan jiǎozi. Wǒ gèng
    xǐhuan jiāngsūcài. Wǒmen chī
    jiāngsūcài, hǎo ma?
  ◆ Hǎo zhǔyi. Wǒ hěn xǐhuan
    jiāngsūcài.
  *They decide on jiāngsūcài (Jiangsu
  cuisine).*

3 ● Nǐmen hǎo. Nǐmen jǐ wèi?
  ◆ Liǎng wèi.
  ● Qǐng zuò.
  ◆ Nǐmen hǎo. Nǐmen jǐ wèi?
  ● Wǒmen liù wèi.
  ◆ Qǐng zuò.
  ● Xièxie.
  a two; b six.

4 ● Zhè shì càidān. Nǐmen xiǎng hē
    shénme?
  ◆ Wǒ hē chá.
  ● Wǒ yě yīyàng.
  ◆ Wǒ gèng xǐhuan píjiǔ.
  ● Dà píng háishi xiǎo píng?
  ● Dà píng, xièxie.
  ● Wǒ yào pútáojiǔ, bái pútáojiǔ.
  *Tea; tea; beer (large bottle); white
  wine.*

Page 89 Understanding what's on the menu

2 *Fish soup, hot & sour soup. Boiled
rice, egg fried rice, stir fried noodles.
Sweet & sour chicken; stir fried lamb,
roast duck, beef curry, marinated
tofu, sweet & sour spare ribs, seasonal
vegetables, sautéed broccoli with
mushrooms.*

Page 90 Ordering a meal

2 ● Nǐmen diǎn cài ma?

◆ Diǎn.
● Zhǔcài yào shénme?
◆ Zhǔcài wǒmen yào yī ge tángcù
  páigǔ, yī ge gālí jīròu, liǎng zhī
  Běijīng kǎoyā, yī ge shícài.
● Zhǔshí yào shénme?
◆ Wǒmen dōu yào bái mǐfàn.
◆ Wǒ gèng xǐhuan dàn chǎofàn.
◆ Wǒ yào chǎomiàn.
● Nàme, qǐng lái yī wǎn dàn chǎofàn,
  yī wǎn chǎomiàn, sì wǎn mǐfàn.
*1 sweet & sour spare ribs, 1 chicken
curry, 2 Beijing roast ducks, 1 seasonal
vegetables; 1 bowl egg fried rice, 1
bowl stir fried noodles, 4 bowls boiled
rice.*

3 ● Wǒ bù chī ròu - wǒ chī sù. Zhè ge
    cài yǒu méi yǒu ròu?
  ◆ Yǒu. Nín chī dàn ma?
  ● Bù chī dàn. Lǔshuǐ dòufu là bú là?
  ◆ Bú là, bú là.
  ● Nàme, qǐng lái yī ge lǔshuǐ dòufu,
    xièxie.
  *Chīsù means vegetarian. She orders
  marinated tofu.*

4 ● Amanda, nǐ xǐhuan mǐjiǔ?
  ◆ Wǒ bú zhīdào.
  ● Fúwùyuán, qǐng lái yī píng **mǐjiǔ**,
    zài lái yī ge **chāzi**. Xièxie.
  ◆ Gěi nín. Mànmàn chī.
  ● Gān bēi.
  He asks for rice wine and a fork.

Page 91 Expressing appreciation

2 ● Gòu ma? Hái yào biéde ma?
  ◆ Gòu le, xièxie. Tíng Huà, gòu ma?
  ● **Gòu le, gòu le.** Hěn hǎochī.
  ◆ Jiàn Zhōng, nǐ chī bǎo le ma?
  ● **Wǒ chī bǎo le, xièxie.**
  ◆ Amanda, nǐ chī bǎo le ma?
  ● **Wǒ chī bǎo le**, fàncài hěn hǎochī.
    Tài hǎo le!

3 ● Fàncài zěnme yàng?
  ◆ **Fàncài hěn hǎochī**, xièxie.
  ● Kǎoyā **fēicháng hǎo, tài hǎo le!**
  ◆ Qǐng jiézhàng.

- Qǐng shāo děng ... Gěi nín.
- Jīntiān wǒ qǐngkè.
- Xièxie.
- Zàijiàn!

Page 92 Put it all together

1 g; h; c; d; a; f; e; b.

2 *a* wǒ bù xǐhuan yú; *b* wǒ bù chī yú; *c* wǒ gèng xǐhuan yú; *d* wǒ hěn xǐhuan yú; *e* yú tài hǎo le; *f* zhè ge yú là ma.

3 *a* seafood soup; *b* beef soup; *c* sweet & sour pork; *d* stir fried vegetables and tofu; *e* lamb curry; *f* deep fried prawns; *g* tomato and egg soup; *h* fried eggs.

4 *a* Wǒ xǐhuan yuècài; *b* Nǐ xǐhuan mǐjiǔ ma?; *c* Wǒ gèng xǐhuan píjiǔ; *d* Wǒmen dōu hěn xǐhuan Zhōngcān.

Page 93 Now you're talking

1
- Huānyíng guānglín. Qǐng wèn, jǐ wèi.
- **Liǎng wèi.**
- Qǐng zuò. Nǐmen yào hē shénme?
- **Wǒmen dōu hē chá, xièxie.**
- Zhè shì càidān.
- **Xièxie.**
- Nǐmen diǎncài ma?
- **Yī ge chǎo niúròu hé yī zhī kǎoyā.**
- Zhǔshí yào shénme?
- **Yī wǎn mǐfàn hé yī wǎn miàntiáo.**
- Nǐmen yào kuàizi háishi chāzi?
- **Kuàizi, xièxie.**
- Gěi nín – yī ge chǎo niúròu hé yī zhī kǎoyā, mǐfàn, miàntiáo. Hái yào biéde ma?
- **Qǐng lài liǎng píng píjiǔ.**
- Hǎo. Mànmàn chī.
- Fàncài zěnmeyàng?
- **Fàncài hěn hǎochī.**
- **Qǐng jiézhàng.**
- Qǐng shāo děng.

Page 94 Quiz

1 sì wèi; *2* No, it's braised lamb; *3* Fúwùyuán!; *4* dòuyá, the others are seafood; *5* western food; *6 a* What would you like as a staple? *b* What is there/have you got as a staple?; *7* Yú xiāng niúròu là bú là?; *8* Gālì niúròu yǒu méi yǒu guǒrén?

Checkpoint 3

Pages 95-98

1 *b* Duìbuqǐ, zuìjìn de jiǔbā zài nǎr?

2 Nín hǎo. Nín hē shénme?
Yī píng píjiǔ.
Xiǎo de háishi dà de?
Dà de, xièxie.
Duōshao qián?
Èrshísì yuán.
Change: qīshíliù yuán.

3 *a* Cèsuǒ zài nǎr?; *b* Fùjìn yǒu méi yǒu wǎngbā?; *c* Yóujú jīntiān kāimén ma?; *d* Qù Xin Gang Wan Fàndiàn zěnme zǒu?

4
- Qù Xin Gang Wan Fàndiàn zěnme zǒu?
- Wǎng běi zǒu. Zǒu dào hónglǜdēng, wǎng zuǒ guǎi, yìzhí zǒu dào dì yī ge lùkǒu, wǎng yòu guǎi. Fàndiàn zài nǐde yòu biān.

Go north. Go to the traffic lights, turn left, go straight on as far as the first crossroads, turn right. The hotel's on your right.

5 *a* **Xīngqīsì** qù Dàlián de **huǒchē** jǐ diǎn kāi?; *b* Huǒchē jǐ diǎn **dào** Dàlián?; *c* Duō shǎo qián yī zhāng **wǎngfǎn** piào?

6 *d* Wǒ yùdìng le yī ge xīngqī de dānrén jiān dài yùshì.

7
- Nǐ hǎo. Wǒ yùdìng le yī ge xīngqī de dānrén jiān dài yùshì.
- Xiānsheng, huānyíng guānglín. Nín guìxìng? Qǐng gěi wǒ nínde hùzhào ... Xièxie. Gěi nín yàoshi – nínde

fángjiān hàomǎ shì èr bā sì jiǔ.
Diàntī zài nínde zuǒ biān.

a surname; b passport; c 2849;
d on the left.

8 ● Nín hǎo. Nín mǎi shénme?
◆ **Wǒ xiǎng mǎi shǒutíbāo.**
● Zhè ge hěn piàoliang. Zhè shì zhēn
pí.
◆ **Tài dà le. Wǒ kěyǐ kànkan nà ge
ma?**
● Gěi nín. Zhè ge yě hěn piàoliang.
Bú dà.
◆ **Wǒ hěn xǐhuan. Duōshao qián?**
● Yī qiān èr bǎi yuán.
◆ **Tài guì le. Bā bǎi zěnmeyàng?**
● Hǎo ba.
◆ **Wǒ kěyǐ yòng xìnyòngka fù ma?**
● Duìbuqǐ, bù kěyǐ.

9 *a* Wǒ jiào Tanaka Keiko; *b* Bú shì, wǒ
shì Rìběnrén.

10 *a* Nǐ zhù zài nǎr?; *b* Nǐ zuò shénme
gōngzuò?; *c* Nǐ jiéhūn le ma?; *d* Nǐ
yǒu háizi ma?; *e* Tā jǐ suì le?; *f* Nǐ
huì shuō Yīngwén ma?; *g* Nǐ xǐhuan
Běijīng cài ma?

Nǐ xìng shénme?; Nǐ jiào shénme?;
Nǐ shì Měiguórén ma?; Nǐ zhù zài
nǎr?; Nǐ zuò shénme gōngzuò?; Nǐ
duō dà le?; Nǐ jiéhūn le ma?; Nǐ yǒu
háizi ma?; Nǐ shuō Fǎwén ma?; Nǐ
xǐhuan chuāncài ma?; Nǐde diànhuà
hàomǎ shì shénme?

11 Míngtiān hé xīngqī'èr wǒ zài Běijīng
gōngzuò. Xīngqī'èr wǎnshang wǒ
qù Dàlián, wǒ zài Dàlián gōngzuò
zhídào xīngqīsì xiàwǔ. Xīngqīsì
wǎnshang hé xīngqīwǔ wǒ zāi
Jǐnzhōu. Xīngqīliù wǒ qù Rìběn
Dōngjīng … wǒde jiā!

Monday & Tuesday: Beijing. Tuesday
evening: Dalian. Wednesday &
Thursday morning: Dalian. Thursday
evening & Friday: Jinzhou. Saturday:
Japan –Tokyo.

12 *a* yú xiāng niúròu; *b* yóumèn dàxiā;
c dòufu shāo yú; *d* Běijīng kǎoyā;
e qīngzhēng quánjī.

f **niúròu dùn tǔdòu** *braised beef with*
potatoes; g **píjiǔ jī** *stewed chicken*
in beer; h **kǎo yáng tuǐ** *roast lamb*
leg; i **yějūn shāo dòufu** *braised tofu*
with mushrooms; j **dòufu shāo yú**
fried fish with tofu; k **shāguō yútóu**
casseroled fish head; l **zhūròu dùn**
fěntiáo *braised pork with noodles;*
m **gān guō jī** *griddle cooked chicken*
with pepper; n **xīhú cù yú** *west lake*
fish in vinegar; o **shuàn yángròu**
Mongolian lamb hotpot.

Chinese characters

English and Chinese systems of writing are based on fundamentally different concepts. English uses an alphabet of letters which represent sounds and which link together to form words. Chinese uses characters which represent meanings – some of them indicate objects and ideas while others indicate pronunciation or grammatical structure.

The characters date back thousands of years. Early characters were simple pictographs representing objects, and many everyday words retain this basic notion although today's versions are much more sophisticated.

人　**rén** *man*
木　**mù** *wood*
口　**kǒu** *mouth*
目　**mù** *eye*
日　**rì** *sun*
月　**yuè** *moon*
雨　**yǔ** *rain*

As well as simple characters, there are more complex ones, which represent ideas and sounds as well as objects.

坐　**zuò** *sit*: two people sitting back to back
明　**míng** *bright*: the sun and moon together
雪　**xuě** *snow*: falling like rain but with ice
吗　**ma**: this shows that a question is being asked; a fusion of *mouth* (indicating *asking*) and a guide to pronunciation

The Chinese language is called **Zhōngwén**. The characters are the same throughout China, understood and used everywhere. However, different branches of Chinese, such as Mandarin, Cantonese and Wu, use different words to interpret them when speaking, to the extent that the spoken languages are not mutually understood.

This book focuses on Mandarin Chinese, which is known as **Pǔtōnghuà** *common language* in mainland China, **Guóyǔ** *national language* in Taiwan and **Huáyǔ** *Chinese language* in Singapore and Malaysia.

pinyin

Chinese characters can't be read by spelling them out, and an official system called **pinyin** has been developed, which uses Roman script (the letters used in English and other western European languages), together with marks to denote tones, to represent the sounds of Mandarin Chinese. **Pinyin** is increasingly widely used, both within China and internationally.

Even though **pinyin** may look like English and many letters sound very similar, it's not an English system and the sounds represented by the letters and the tone marks need to be learnt. Some of the most striking differences in the consonants are:

c sounds like the English *ts* in pa*ts*
q sounds a bit like the English *ch* in *ch*ip
x sounds a bit like the English *sh* in *sh*ip
(For more on pronunciation, see page 6.)

structure

Each character represents a syllable. Some Chinese words are a single character:

好 **hǎo** *good*
国 **guó** *country*
人 **rén** *person*

others are made up of two or more characters:

你好 **nǐhǎo** *hello*, literally *you good*
好吃 **hàochī** *delicious*, literally *good eating*
好看 **hǎokàn** *good looking*
好听 **hǎotīng** *nice to listen to*, literally *good hearing*

中国 **Zhōngguó** *Chinese*; **zhōng** means *the middle*, so literally *middle country (Middle Kingdom)*
中国人 **Zhōngguórén** *Chinese*, literally *middle country person*
英国 **Yīngguó** *UK*; **yīng** is the phonetic version of the first syllable of England plus *country*
英国人 **Yīngguórén** *British*, literally *UK person*
美国 **Měiguó** *USA*; **měi** is a phonetic version of the second syllable of America plus *country*
美国人 **Měiguórén** *American*, literally *USA person*

grammar

When we talk, we do more than just say words randomly; we use them in a specific order and they relate to one another. Grammar is the explanation of how that works – and getting to grips with Chinese grammar rules will be easier if 1) you're familiar with basic grammar terminology and 2) you're prepared for the main differences between how Chinese and English work.

essential grammatical terms

Nouns are the words for living beings, things, places and abstract concepts: *woman*, *son*, *doctor*, *Henry*, *dog*, *table*, *house*, *China*, *time*, *joy*, *freedom*.

Singular means one; **plural** means more than one.

Pronouns are words that can replace nouns. The most commonly used pronouns are **personal pronouns**, e.g. *you, she, him, we, it, they, them*.

Adjectives are words that describe nouns and pronouns: <u>good</u> *food*; <u>strong</u> <u>red</u> *wine*; <u>my</u> *car*; *I am* <u>tired</u>; *it was* <u>superb</u>.

Adverbs add information to verbs, adjectives, other adverbs and whole sentences: *he's acting* <u>weirdly</u>; <u>very</u> *good idea;* <u>luckily</u> *he's not here*.

Prepositions are words like *in*, *at*, *beside*, *from*, *over*, *before*, which usually have a noun or a pronoun after them.

Verbs are words like *go*, *sleep*, *eat*, *like*, *have*, *be*, *live*, *die*, that relate to doing and being.

The **subject** of a sentence is the person/thing carrying out the verb: e.g. <u>the girl</u> *is eating an apple*.

The **object** of a sentence is the person/thing having the verb done to it, e.g. *the girl is eating* <u>an apple</u>.

A **negative** sentence uses *not* with the verb.

basic differences between Chinese and English grammar

- Word order is a very important feature of Chinese. It is not flexible as it often is in English; there are fixed rules governing the order in which words and expressions appear in a sentence.

- Chinese has no words for *a*, *the* or *some*: **chá** means *tea*, *a tea*, *the tea* or *some tea*. The meaning is understood from the context.

- English nouns have a plural form, most add *s* or *es*, e.g. *cat/cats*, *bus/buses*, while others undergo a different change, e.g. *man/men*, *mouse/mice*. Chinese singular and plural nouns are exactly the same, and rely on the context to make the meaning clear.

- Verbs too have only one form in Chinese. Where English has *eat*, *eats*, *eating*, *ate*, *has eaten*, *will eat*, Chinese has **chī**. The various different meanings are conveyed via other words in the sentence.

G1   word order

Word order in simple short sentences is as in English:

subject + **verb** + object
Wǒ hē chá. *I drink tea.*
Tā chī mǐfàn. *She eats rice.*
Lǐ Wěi jiāo Zhōngwén. *Lǐ Wěi teaches Chinese.*

Information about when, where and how something happens comes before the verb:

subject + **when** + verb + object
Tā měi tiān jiāo Zhōngwén. *He teaches Chinese every day.*
Wǒmen xīngqí'èr zǒu. *We are leaving on Tuesday.*

subject + **where** + verb + object
Tā zài xiǎoxué jiāo Zhōngwén. *He teaches Chinese at primary school.*
Wǒ zài shāngdiàn mǎi dōngxī. *I buy things at the shop.*

subject + **how** + verb+ object
Tā mànman de chī mǐfàn. *She eats rice slowly.*
Wǒ hěn xǐhuān chuāncài. *I like Sichuan food very much.*

When there's information about both time and place, *when* comes before *where*:

when + subject + **where** + verb + object
Míngtiān wǒ zài kāfēi tīng jiàn nǚ péngyou. *I am meeting my girlfriend in the café tomorrow.*

Descriptions of time/place go from the largest unit to the smallest:

Míngtiān xiàwǔ sān diǎn wǒ zài kāfēi tīng jiàn nǚ péngyǒu. *I'm meeting my girlfriend in the café at three o'clock tomorrow.* (Lit. *Tomorrow afternoon three o'clock I at the café meet my girl friend.*)

This applies to dates and addresses:

èr líng yī sì *2014* **bāyuè** *August* **èrshí'èr hào** *22nd* **xīngqīwǔ** *Friday*, i.e. *Friday, 22 August 2014*
Jiāngsū 215227 Wújiāng, Zhāng Huà Lù 453 *453 Zhang Hua Road, Wujiang, 215227 Jiangsu*

Question words don't appear at the beginning of a question. Instead, they go in the same place as where the answer would be:

Zhè shì <u>wǒ péngyou</u> *This is <u>my friend</u>.*
Zhè shì <u>shuí</u>? *This is <u>who</u>? i.e. Who is this?*

(see **G10 Questions**)

G2 nouns

Nouns don't have a plural form – they're the same in both singular and plural, and rely on the context to make the meaning clear:

Zhè shì wǒde péngyou Xǔ Qīng. *This is my friend Xǔ Qīng.*
Wǒ yǒu hěnduō péngyou. *I have many friends.*

Yǒu cānguǎn. *There's a restaurant.*
Yǒu wǔ jiā cānguǎn. *There are five restaurants.*

Chinese has no words for *the* or *a/an*:

Cèsuǒ zài <u>lóuxià</u>. *(The) toilet is downstairs.*
Gōngyuán lí zhèr yuǎn ma? *Is (the) park far from here?*
Wǒ shì xuésheng. *I'm (a) student.*

If *a/an* is used to indicate *one*, you can use **yī** + measure word + noun.
Yǒu yī jiā cānguǎn. *There's a restaurant.* (i.e. only the one)
(see **G8 Measure words**)

G3 personal pronouns

Personal pronouns (*I, she, us, they,* etc.) are the same in Chinese whether they're the subject or the object of a sentence.

wǒ *I, me*	**wǒmen** *we, us*
nǐ/nín *you*	**nǐmen** *you* (more than one person)
tā *he/she, him/her*	**tāmen** *they, them*

Wǒ ài nǐ. *I love you.*
Nǐ ài wǒ. *You love me.*

Wǒmen qǐng tāmen. *We invite them.*
Tāmen qǐng wǒmen. *They invite us.*

Nín is more formal than **nǐ** and is often used to address customers in shops or restaurants, and to show respect towards senior people in business or the elderly.

G4 possession

Possession is indicated with **de**:

Xuán de chē *Xuán's car*
gōngsī de zǒngbù *the company('s) headquarters*
Shànghǎi de huǒchē *the Shanghai train*
wǒde gōngyù *my flat*

- **de** can be omitted when there's a close personal connection:
  wǒ māma/wǒde māma *my mother*
  nǐ jiā/nǐde jiā *your home*
- **wǒde, nǐde, tāde, wǒmende, nǐmende** and **tāmende** can mean both *my* and *mine, your* and *yours,* etc.
  Zhè shì tāde gōngyù. *This is his/her flat.* **Zhè shì wǒde.** *This is mine.*

G5 adjectives

With a noun, adjectives of one syllable are used as in English:

xiǎo gōngyù *small flat*   **dà fángzi** *big house*

But when a description involves more than one syllable or an adverb, **de** is added:

xiàndài de gōngyù *modern flat*   **hěndà de fángzi** *very big house*

- **De** added to an adjective without a noun means *one(s)*:
  xiǎo de *the small one(s);* **dà de** *the big one(s);* **hóng de** *the red one(s)*
- **Tài** + adjective + **le** means *too* or *extremely*:
  tàiguì le *too expensive;* **tàixiǎo le** *tiny*
- **Shì** *to be* is not used with adjectives:
  Gōngyù tǐng xiǎo. *The flat (is) rather small.*

Fángzi hěn lǎo. *The house (is) very old.*
Nǐ lèi/máng ma? *(Are) you tired/busy?*
Wǒ bú lèi. *I (am) not tired.* **Tā tǐng máng.** *He (is) rather busy.*

This does not apply to describing nationality, e.g. **Tā shì Zhōngguórén** *He is Chinese,* because **Zhōngguórén** means *a Chinese person.*

G6 zài

The preposition **zài** can mean *to/in/at*:

Wǒ zhù zài Běijīng. *I live in Beijing.*
Wǒ zài fēijīchǎng gōngzuò. *I work at the airport.*

Zài is also a verb meaning *to be in/at/on*, so **shì** isn't needed with it:

Shànghǎi zài Zhōngguó. *Shanghai is in China.*
Fēijīchǎng zài Pǔdōng. *The airport is in Pudong.*
Diàntī zài zuǒ biān. *The lift is on the left.*

Quite unrelated to the above, **zài** before a verb means that someone is in the process of doing something:

Tā zài dú. *She's reading right now.*
Wǒmen zài mǎi dōngxī. *We're buying things.*

G7 numbers

Numbers are set out on pages 19 and 26.
- In lists of numbers, *one* is pronounced **yāo**, not **yī**.
- **Liǎng** is used instead of **èr** when talking about two of something: **Wǒ yǒu liǎng ge érzi.** *I have two sons.*
- **Bǎifēnzhī** *percent* goes before the number: **bǎifēnzhī wǔshí** *50%.*
- Putting **dì** before a number turns it into an ordinal e.g: **dì yī** *first*, **dì èr** *second*, **dì sān** *third*, **dì shí** *tenth*, **dì èrshíwǔ** *25th*

G8 measure words

A noun cannot come directly after a number or after **nà/zhè** *that/this*. A measure word (MW) has to come between them, and this categorises the noun that follows.

There are around 50 MWs, the most common being **ge**, used for people – **sān ge péngyou** *three friends* – and also as the default option for things that don't fall within other categories, e.g. **bā ge yuè** *eight months.*

Some MWs equate to English concepts:
zhè bēi kāfēi *this <u>cup</u> of coffee*
liǎng píng shuǐ *two <u>bottles</u> of water*

nà guàn píjiǔ *that <u>can</u> of beer*
sān bāo miàntiáo *three <u>packets</u> of noodles*

Others have no equivalent and are not translated, e.g:

books: **zhè běn cídiǎn** *this dictionary*; **nà běn shū** *that book*
vehicles: **liǎng liàng chē** *two cars*; **sān liàng gōnggòng qìchē** *three buses*
business: **nà jiā cānguǎn** *that restaurant*; **zhè jiā yínháng** *this bank*
long items of clothing: **liǎng tiáo lǐngdài** *two ties*; **yī tiáo kùzi** *one pair of trousers*
large animals: **yī tóu dà xiàng** *one elephant*; **sì tóu niú** *four cows*
flat paper items: **sān zhāng piào** *three tickets*; **yì zhāng dìtú** *one map*
birds: **nà zhī jī** *that chicken*; **zhè zhī yāzi** *this duck*
huge things: **nà zuò shān** *that mountain*; **zhè zuò chéngshì** *this city*

MWs are also used with ordinal numbers: **dìwǔ běn shū** *the fifth book*.
However, they're not used with **tiān** *day* and **nián** *year*, or with units of measurement, e.g. **jīn** *500 g*, **gōnglǐ** *km*.

G9   verbs

Verbs, words like *to be, to live, to play, to understand, to have,* which refer to doing and being, have only one form, regardless of who the subject is:

wǒ qù *I go*
wǒmen qù *we go*
tā qù *he/she goes*

Even when there are two verbs together, there's only the one form:

wǒ yào qù *I want to go*
wǒ bìxū qù *I have to go*
wǒ néng qù *I can go/I'm capable of going*
wǒ kěyǐ qù *I can go/I'm allowed to go*
wǒ huì yóuyǒng *I can swim/I know how to swim*
wǒ xǐhuan yóuyǒng *I like to swim/swimming*

To make a sentence negative in the present tense, you put **bù** before the verb: **wǒ bú qù** *I don't go/I'm not going*; **wǒ bú huì yóuyǒng** *I can't swim*; **tā bú chī mǐfàn** *She doesn't eat rice.*

The only exception is **yǒu**, which means *have* as well as *there is/are.* In the negative it becomes **méi yǒu**.
Wǒ yǒu yīngbàng; méi yǒu rénmínbì. *I have British pounds; I don't have RMB.*
Lóuxià yǒu nán cèsuǒ; méi yǒu nǚ cèsuǒ. *Downstairs there is a gents; there's no ladies.*

Repeating a verb introduces a casual note, e.g. **liáoliao** *chat*:
Wǒ lái jièshao jièshao … *Let me introduce …*
Wǒmen shuōshuo. *We'll have a word.*
Tā xiǎngxiang. *She's thinking it over.*
Shìshi zhè jiàn máoyī. *Try this sweater.*
Qǐng nǐ chángchang wǒ zuò de cài. *Please taste the dish I cooked.*

Other useful everyday verbs include **zuò** *sit*, **zhàn** *stand*, **zǒu** *walk*, **pǎo** *run*, **tīng** *listen*, **kàn** *watch*, **shuō** *speak*, **xiě** *write*, **chī** *eat*, **hē** *drink*, **zhù** *live*, **mǎi** *buy*, **lái** *come*, **shuìjiào** *sleep*, **dú** *read*, **dǒng** *understand*, **xiào** *laugh*.

G10 questions

Questions words, e.g. **shéi** (or **shuí**) *who*, **shénme** *what* or **duōshǎo** *how many,* go in the same position as the answer will be:

Zhè shì <u>shuí</u>? *Who is this?* (Lit. *This is who?*)
Zhè shì <u>wǒ māma</u>. *This is my mother.*

Nǐ hē <u>shénme</u>? *What are you drinking?* (Lit. *You drink what?*)
Wǒ hē <u>shuǐ</u>. *I'm drinking water.*

Nín yào <u>duōshǎo</u> píngguǒ? *How many apples do you want?* (Lit. *You want how many apples?*)
Wǒ yào <u>shí'èr gè</u> píngguǒ. *I want twelve apples.*

Other questions words include **nǎr** (or **nǎli**) *where*, **shénme shíhou** *when*, **nǎ** *which*, **jǐdiǎn** *what time*, **zěnme** *how*, **zěnmeyàng** *how about*, **duōshǎo qián** *how much*, **jǐdiǎn** *what time*.

Since information about time/place goes before the verb (**G1**), any related question words go there too:

Nǐ <u>shénme shíhou</u> qù Běijīng? *When are you going to Beijing?* (Lit. *You when go Beijing?*)
Wǒ <u>míngtiān</u> qù Běijīng. *I'm going to Beijing tomorrow.* (Lit. *I tomorrow go Beijing.*)

Huǒchē <u>jǐ diǎn</u> kāi. *What time does the train depart?* (Lit. *The train what time departs?*)
Huǒchē <u>xiàwǔ sān</u> diǎn kāi. *The train departs at 3 p.m.*

There are two ways of asking yes/no questions:

1 Adding **ma** to the end of a statement:
  Tā shì lǎoshī. *He is a teacher.* **Tā shì lǎoshī ma?** *Is he a teacher?*
  Nǐ hē chá. *You drink tea.* **Nǐ hē chá ma?** *Do you drink tea?*
  Tā chī mǐfàn. *She eats rice.* **Tā chī mǐfàn ma?** *Does she eat rice?*

2 Repeating the verb or adjective, adding **bù** in the middle:

Tā shì bú shì lǎoshī? *Is he a teacher?*
Nǐ hē bù hē chá? *Do you drink tea?*
Yángròu là bú là? *Is the lamb spicy?*

The only exception is **yǒu**, which adds **méi**:

Yǒu méi yǒu cānguǎn? *Is there a restaurant?*

In questions offering alternatives, *or* is **háishi**. **Ma** is not used:

Nǐ yào chá háishi kāfēi? *Would you like tea or coffee?*

G11 answers

There's no catch-all translation for *yes* and *no*. Generally the verb or the adjective of the question is used in the answer:

Nǐ shì lǎoshī ma? *Are you a teacher?* **Shì** *Yes*; **Bú shì** *No*
Nǐmen hē bù hē kāfēi? *Do you drink coffee?* **Hē** *Yes*; **Bù hē** *No*
Nǐ zhīdào dìzhǐ ma? *Do you know the address?* **Zhīdào** *Yes*; **Bù zhīdào** *No*
Nǐ xǐhuan hǎixiān ma? *Do you like seafood?* **Xǐhuan** *Yes*; **Bù xǐhuan** *No*
Tā huì bú huì yóuyǒng? *Can he swim?* **Huì** *Yes*; **Bú huì** *No*
Nǐ lèi ma? *Are you tired.* **Hěn lèi** *Yes, very*; **Bú lèi** *No*
Tāmen yǒu piào ma? *Do they have tickets?* **Yǒu** *Yes*; **Méi yǒu** *No*
De can be added to **shì** for emphasis:
Nǐ shì Chang ma? *Are you Chang?* **Shì, shìde.** *Yes, yes I am.*

G12 le

Le, which has no direct equivalent in English, has many functions, including the following:

- With **tài** and an adjective it means *extremely* or *too*:
  tài dà le *extremely/too big*
- At the end of a sentence, it indicates that a situation has changed:
  Wǒ líhūn le. *I'm divorced.*
  Wǒ méi yǒu qián le. *I've no money (left).*
- After a verb, it shows that the action occurred in the past:
  Wǒ qù le Zhōngguó. *I went to China./I've been to China.*
  Tā mǎi le yī liàng chē. *He bought a car.*

> **Chī le ma?** which means *Have you eaten?* is used as a greeting in some parts of China.

wordpower

Knowledge of grammatical structures has a key place in learning a new language but is of limited use without a good stock of words to slot into those structures.

There are various ways of acquiring vocabulary. It's generally easier to remember words when you come across and use them in context. You'll probably find that you associate certain linguistic structures with the vocabulary from the same **Talk Mandarin Chinese** unit, e.g. in Unit 7 **Wǒ zài zhǎo …** *I'm looking for …* is linked with **lǐngdài** *tie* and **pījiān** *pashmina*. Using **Wǒ zài zhǎo …** with other items both practises the phrase and broadens vocabulary.

The categories below can be practised with any relevant key phrases from the book. Clothing links with liking and colours as well as shopping; liking can also be used to talk about sports. Simple descriptive sentences can be created using the lists of adjectives – all you need is the person/place and the adjective, e.g. **Tā piàoliang.** *She is beautiful.*

---

adjectives describing people: gèzi gāo *tall*, **gèzi ǎi** *short*, **pàng** *fat*, **shòu** *thin*, **tóufa zháng** *long hair*, **tóufa duǎn** *short hair*, **yǎnjīng dà** *big eyes*, **yǎnjīng xiǎo** *small eyes*, **piàoliang** *beautiful*, **shuài** *handsome*, **kù** *cool*

adjectives describing places: dà *big*, **xiǎo** *small*, **gānjing** *clean*, **zàng** *dirty*, **ānjing** *quiet*, **rènao** *lively*, **yǒngjǐ** *crowded*, **yǒu lìshǐ** *historic*, **yǒumíng** *famous*

colours: hóngsè *red*, **lánsè** *blue*, **huángsè** *yellow*, **lǜsè** *green*, **hēisè** *black*, **báisè** *white*, **fěnhóngsè** *pink*, **zōngsè** *brown*, **huīsè** *grey*, **zǐsè** *purple*

clothing: dàyī *coat*, **fēngyī** *windbreaker*, **máoyī** *sweater*, **jiákè** *jacket*, **tángzhuāng** *traditional Chinese costume*, **xīzhuāng** *suit*, **chènshān** *shirt*, **tì xù** *t shirt*, **kùzi** *trousers*, **niúzǎikù** *jeans*, **qúnzi** *skirt*, **liányīqún** *dress*

sports: wǎngqiú *tennis*, **lánqiú** *basketball*, **páiqiú** *volleyball*, **yǔmáoqiú** *badminton*, **pīngpāng qiú** *table tennis*, **zúqiú** *football*, **yóuyǒng** *swimming*, **tiàoshuǐ** *diving*, **huábīng** *skating*, **huáxuě** *skiing*

animals: shīzi *lion*, **bàozi** *leopard*, **lǎohǔ** *tiger*, **dàxiàng** *elephant*, **xióng** *bear*, **xióngmāo** *panda*, **lù** *deer*, **yáng** *sheep*, **zhū** *pig*, **jī** *chicken*, **yā** *duck*, **māo** *cat*, **gǒu** *dog*

festivals: chūnjié *Spring Festival*, **yuánxiāo jié** *Lantern Festival*, **qīngmíng jié** *Ching Ming Festival*, **duānwǔ jié** *Dragon Boat Festival*, **qīxì jié** *Tanabata Festival*, **zhōngqiū jié** *Mid-Autumn Festival*

Using the structure **Wǒ xīgài téng** *My knee is hurting*/**Wǒ jiǎo téng**
My feet are hurting, practise with a few other parts of the body: **bízi** *nose*,
yǎnjīng *eyes*, **zuǐ** *mouth*, **ěrduǒ** *ears*, **méimáo** *eyebrows*, **liǎn** *face*, **yá**
teeth, **tóu** *head*, **gēbó** *arms*, **tuǐ** *legs*, **shǒu** *hands*, **jiǎo** *feet*, **wèi** *stomach*,
dùzi *tummy*, **xīn** *heart*, **gān** *liver*, **fèi** *lungs*, **shèn** *kidney*, **dǎn** *gall bladder*.

Some words are the basis of associated words. Knowing this can help
you remember them.

diàn *electricity*
diàndēng *electric light, light*
diànnǎo *computer*, lit. *electronic brain*
diànhuà *telephone*, lit. *electronic talk*
diànshì *TV*, lit. *electronic vision*
diànyǐng *movies*, lit. *electronic shadows*
diànchē *tram*, lit. *electric bus*
diàntī *lift, elevator*, lit. *electric stairs*
diànshàn *electric fan*

bāo *bag*
bēibāo *rucksack*, lit. *back bag*
qiánbāo *wallet*, lit. *money bag*
shǒutíbāo *handbag*, lit. *hand carrying bag*
shūbāo *school bag*, lit. *book bag*
lǚxíng bāo *travel bag*, lit. *travel bag*

xié *shoes*
píxié *leather shoes*
yùndòng xié *sports shoes*
xiūxián xié *casual shoes*
liángxié *sandals*
tuōxié *slippers*
gāogēnxié *high heels*

jī *machine*
fādòngjī *engine*
fēijī *plane*
diànshìjī *TV set*
shōuyīnjī *radio*
shǒujī *mobile phone*
ěrjī *headset*
dǎyìnjī *printer*
dìng shū jī *stapler*

guǎn *an indoor place for activities*
dàshǐ guǎn *embassy*
lǐngshìguǎn *consulate*
bīnguǎn *hotel*
cānguǎn *restaurant*
fànguǎn *restaurant*
cháguǎn *teahouse*
jiǔguǎn *pub*
kāfēi guǎn *café*
měishù guǎn *art gallery*
zhǎnlǎn guǎn *exhibition*
tǐyùguǎn *stadium*
túshū guǎn *library*
lǐfǎ guǎn *barber's*
bówùguǎn *museum*

jiǔ *alcoholic drink*
mǐjiǔ *rice wine*
pútáojiǔ *wine*
píngguǒ jiǔ *cider*
báijiǔ *liquor*
máotái jiǔ *maotai*
píjiǔ *beer*
xiāngbīnjiǔ *champagne*
lán mǔ jiǔ *rum*

Not all alcoholic drinks include **jiǔ**: **báilándì** brandy, **wēishìjì** whiskey, **fútèjiā** vodka.

Last, but certainly not least, consider the vocabulary that's particularly relevant to your life and your lifestyle. A good place to start is a dictionary, whether a book or online. As you come across new words that interest you, jot them down on the next page and practise saying them with some of the *Top Ten Essentials* on page 132.

top ten essentials

1 Talking about people:
   Wǒ shì yīngguó rén. *I am English.*
   Zhè shì wǒ bàba hé māma. *This is my dad and mum.*
   Nǐ bú shì xuéshēng. *You are not a student.*

2 Talking about having:
   Wǒ yǒu yīngbàng. *I have pounds.*
   Wǒ méi yǒu rénmínbì. *I don't have RMB.*

3 Talking about what's available:
   Yǒu cānguǎn. *There is a restaurant./There are (some) restaurants.*
   Yǒu yínháng ma? *Is there a bank?/Are there (any) banks?*
   Méi yǒu shāngdiàn. *There is/are no shop(s).*

4 Asking where things are:
   Cèsuǒ zài nǎr? *Where is/Where are the toilet(s)?*

5 Saying what you like and dislike:
   Wǒ xǐhuān zhè tiáo wéijīn. *I like this scarf.*
   Wǒ xǐhuān xué Zhōngwén. *I like learning Chinese.*
   Wǒ bù xǐhuān zhège yánsè. *I don't like this colour.*

6 Saying you'd like (to do) something:
   Wǒ yào yìbēi lǜchá. *I want/I'd like a cup of green tea.*
   Wǒmen yào huàn qián. *We want/We'd like to change money.*

7 Asking if you can do something:
   Wǒ néng/keyi yòng diànhuà ma? *Can/May I use the phone?*
   Wǒmen néng/keyi zuò zài zhèr ma? *Can/May we sit here?*

8 Asking someone to do something:
   Nǐ néng bù néng bāng wǒ?/Nǐ néng bāng wǒ ma?
   Could you help me?
   Qǐng zài shuō yíbiàn. *Please say it again.*
   Qǐng shuō màn yìdiǎn ... *Please speak more slowly...*
   ... wǒ zhèngzài xué Zhōngwén ... *I'm learning to speak Chinese.*

9 Asking what things are:
   Zhè shì shénme? *What is it?*
   ... Zhōngwén zěnme shuō? *How do you say ... in Chinese?*

10 Saying/asking if you have to do something:
   Wǒ bìxū zǒu le. *I have to/must go.*
   Wǒ bìxū zhème zuò ma? *Do I have to do this?*

Newport Community
Learning & Libraries

Chinese–English glossary

A
Ài'ěrlán Ireland
àiren spouse, partner
Àodàliyà Australia
Àodàliyàrén Australian

B
ba *word used to make suggestions*
bā eight
bàba father
bǎi hundred
bài worship
báicài Chinese leaves
bǎihuò shāngdiàn department store
báilándì brandy
bái (mǐ)fàn boiled (lit. white) rice
bái pútáojiǔ white wine
bái(sè) white
bàn half
bàngōngshì office
bāngzhù help
bāo packet; include
bǎoxiǎnxiāng safe (box)
bāozi steamed bun
bāshí eighty
bāshíqī eighty-seven
bēi glass, cup
běi north
Běijīngrén Beijing person
běn *measure word*
běndìrén local person
biān side
biàn *measure word*
biǎo form
biéde other
bīng ice
bīnguǎn hotel
bǐsà bǐng pizza
bìxū have to, must
bōcài spinach
bōluó pineapple

bówùguǎn museum
bù not
bú kèqi you're welcome
bú xiè you're welcome

C
cài dish
càidān menu
cānguǎn restaurant
céng floor, level
cèsuǒ toilet
chá tea
chà yī kè a quarter to
Chángchéng the Great Wall
chǎo stir fry; noisy
chǎofàn fried rice
chāojí super
chāojí shìchǎng supermarket
chǎomiàn fried noodles
chāzi fork
chē car, vehicle
chéng city
chéngzī orange
chènshān shirt
chēzhàn bus stop
chī eat
chībǎo to be full
chīsù vegetarian
chuāncài Sichuan cuisine
chúnmáo pure wool
chūzūchē taxi
cì *measure word, number of train*
cōng onion
cóng from

D
dà big
dà hào large size
dài with
dàn egg
dānchéng single journey

dānjiān single room
dānrén fángjiān single room
dānshēn single (unmarried)
dànshì but
dāngrán of course
dào arrive
dǎoyóu tour guide
dàxiā prawn
dàxué university
de *word to show possession or to link up a long adjective with a noun*
Déguó Germany
Déguórén German (nationality)
děng wait
Déwén German (language)
dì *prefix in front of a number to make it an ordinal number*
diǎn o'clock
diǎncài order a meal
diànhuà telephone
diànhuà hàomǎ phone number
diàntī lift, escalator
dìdi younger brother
dìtiě underground
dìtú map
dōng east
dǒng understand
dōu all, both
dòufu beancurd
dòuyá beansprout
duì correct
duìbuqǐ sorry
duìmiàn opposite
dùjià on holiday
duō many
duōdà? how old?
duō jiǔ? how long?

duōshao? how many?, how much?

E

é goose
è hungry
èr two
ěrhuán earring
èrshí 20
èryuè February
érzi son

F

Fǎguó France
Fǎguórén French person
fàn rice, meal
fàncài food
fàndiàn restaurant, hotel
fángjiān room
fángshàiyóu suncream
Fǎwén French (language)
Fǎyǔ French (language)
fēicháng very, extremely
Fēilǜbīn The Phillipines
fēn *Chinese currency unit*
fēng wind
fēngshuǐ fengshui (lit. wind and water)
fēngzheng kite
fēnzhōng minute
fù pay
fùjìn nearby
fúwùyuán waiter, waitress
fúzhuāng clothes

G

gālí curry
gān bēi Cheers!
gāoxìng happy
ge *measure word*
gēge elder brother
gěi give; for
gēn with; follow
gèng even, more
gōngchǎng factory
gōngchéngshī engineer
gōngfu martial art

gōnggòng public
gōnggòng qìchē bus
gōnglǐ kilometre
gōngsī company
gōngyì měishù diàn arts and crafts shop
gōngyù flat, apartment
gōngyuán park
gōngzuò work, job
gòu enough
gòuwù zhōngxīn shopping centre
guā melon
guǎi turn
guàn can, tin
guānglín be present
Guǎngzhōurén Guangzhou person
guānmén close
Gùgōng the Forbidden City
guì expensive
guìxìng surname
guó country
guójí nationality
guójiā country
guǒrén nut

H

hái still, in addition
hǎi sea
hǎibiān seaside
háishi or
hǎixiān seafood
háizi child
hán contain, include
hànbǎo bāo hamburger
Hánguó South Korea
Hánguórén Korean (nationality)
hǎo good, well
hào date; number; size
hǎochī delicious (for food)
hǎohē delicious (for drink)
háohuá luxury
hàomǎ number

hē drink
hé and; river
hēi(sè) black
hěn very
hěnduō many
hóng chá black tea
hónglǜdēng traffic light
hóng pútáojiǔ red wine
hóng(sè) red
hóngshāo stewed in dark soy sauce
hòu thick
hòulái late
hú lake
huā chá jasmine tea
huàláng art gallery
huānyíng welcome
huānyíng guānglín welcome
huáng(sè) yellow
huāyuán garden
huí jiàn see you later
huì can, able to
hùliánwǎng internet
huǒchē train
huǒchēzhàn train station
huòzhě or
hùzhào passport

J

jī chicken
jīdàn egg
jī(ròu) chicken meat
jiā family
jiā dà extra large
jiān *measure word*; fried
jiàn *measure word*; to meet
Jiānádàrén Canadian
jiànshēngfáng gym
jiāo teach
jiǎo *Chinese currency unit*
jiào call, be called
jiāoqū suburb
jiàoxǐng wake up
jiǎozi dumpling
jiārén family member
jiātíng family

jiéhūn married
jiějie elder sister
jiēkǒu connection point
jièlán Chinese broccoli
jièshào introduce
jiézhàng to settle the bill
jǐhào what number, what date
jīn *Chinese weight unit, equal to half a kilo*
jìn enter
jīntiān today
jīnglǐ manager
jīnwǎn tonight
jǐ suì how old
jiǔ wine
jiǔbā wine bar
jiǔdiàn hotel
jiǔshí ninety
jiǔyuè September
jìzhě journalist
jú bureau
júhuā chá chrysanthemum tea
gējùyuàn opera house
júzi tangerine
júzi zhī orange juice

K

kǎbùqínuò cappuccino
kāfēi coffee
kāfēiguǎn café
kāi open; leave
kāimén open
kànkan to have a look
Kānpéilā Canberra
kǎo roasted
kǎoyā roast duck
kělè cola
kěyǐ can, may
kòng vacant
kōngtiáo air-conditioning
kuài *Chinese currency unit*
kuàijìshī accountant
kuàizi chopsticks
kuàngquán shuǐ mineral water

L

là spicy hot
lái come
lán(sè) blue
Lánkǎisītè Lancaster
lǎoshī teacher
le *grammatical partical*
lǐ *unit of length, 1 li = 0.5 kilometre*
liàng *measure word*
liǎng two
liǎngrén fángjiān twin room
líhūn divorce
líng zero
lǐngdài tie
liù six
liùshí sixty
lìzhī lychee
lízi pear
lóngxiā lobster
lóushàng upstairs
lóuxià downstairs
lù road, route
lǔcài Shandong cuisine
lǜ chá green tea
lùkǒu crossroad
Lúndūn London
lǜ(sè) green
lǔshuǐ marine sauce, gravy
lǜshī lawyer
lǚxíngshè travel agent
lǚyóu travel, tour
lǚyóujú tourist board

M

ma *question word*
mǎi buy
mài sell
májiàng marjong
Mǎláixīyà Malaysia
māma mother
mǎmǎhūhū so-so
mǎn full
màn slow
mángguǒ mango
mànmàn chī enjoy your meal

máo *Chinese currency unit*
màozi hat, cap
Měiguó America
Měiguórén American (person)
mèimei younger sister
měi tiān every day
méi yǒu do not have
miàn(tiáo) noodles
mǐfàn rice
mì guā melon
mǐjiǔ rice wine
mí lù to be lost
mǐncài Fujian cuisine
míngpiàn name/business card
míngtiān tomorrow
míngxìnpiàn postcard
míngzi name
mínzú nationality
mógu mushroom
mótuōchē motorbike
mùdìdì destination

N

nǎ which
nà that; there
nàbiān over there
nǎ guó rén? what nationality are you?
nǎi chá tea with milk
nǎinai grandmother (on father's side)
nǎli where
nǎli nǎli not at all
nàme then, in that case
nán south; male
Nánjīngrén Nanjing person
nán péngyou boyfriend
nǎr where
ne *grammatical particle*
néng to be able to, can
nǐ you
nián year
nǐde your; yours
nǐ hǎo hello
nǐmen you (plural)

nín you (formal)
nín hǎo hello (formal)
níngméng lemon
niúliǔ sliced beef
niúnǎi milk
niúròu beef
Niǔyuē New York
nóngcūn countryside
nǚ female
nǚ'ér daughter
nǚ péngyou girlfriend
nǚshì madam

P

páigǔ spare ribs
pángbiān next to
péngyou friend
piányi cheap
piào ticket
piàoliang beautiful
pígé leather
pījiān pashmina, shawl
píjiǔ beer
píng bottle
píngguǒ apple
pútáojiǔ wine

Q

qī seven
qiān thousand
qián money
qiǎokèlì chocolate
qìchē automobile
qǐng invite; please
qīngcài green vegetables
qǐngkè to treat
somebody (to a meal)
qīngnián lǚshè youth
hostel
qǐng wèn may I ask?
qīngzhēng steamed
qīshí seventy
qítā other
qù to go

R

ràng to allow
rén person

Rénmínbì (RMB) *Chinese
currency*
rènshi to get to know a
person
Rìběn Japan
Rìběnrén Japanese
(person)
Rìwén Japanese
(language)
Rìyǔ Japanese (language)
ròu meat
ruǎnwò soft sleeper
ruǎnzuò soft seat

S

sān three
sānshí thirty
shān mountain
shāngdiàn shop
Shànghǎirén Shanghai
people
shàngwǔ morning
shàngyī jacket
shānshuǐhuà landscape
painting
shǎo little, few
shāo děng just a minute
sháozi spoon
shēng to be born
shěng province
shénme what
shénme shíhou when
shí ten
shì to be; city; try
shícài seasonal vegetable
shìchǎng market
shìde yes
shí'èryuè December
shíhou time
shìshi to have a try,
try on
shíyīyuè November
shì zhōngxīn town centre
shǒujī mobile phone
shòupiàochù ticket
office
shǒutíbāo handbag
shuāngrén fángjiān
double room

shuǐ water
shuǐguǒ diàn
greengrocer's
shuō speak, say
sī silk
sǐ to die; death
sì four
sìshí forty
sù vegetarian
suàn garlic
suānlà hot and sour
sùcài vegetarian dish
Sūgélán Scotland
Sūgélánrén Scottish
(person)
suì years old
suìshu years old (used
when asking old people
their age)

T

tā he/she/him/her
tài too, extremely
Tàiguó Thailand
tàijí t'ai chi
tàitai wife, Mrs
tāmen they/them
tāmende their/theirs
tāng soup
táng sugar
tángcù sweet and sour
táocí porcelain
táozi peach
tiān day
tóngshì colleague,
workmate
túshūguǎn library

W

wàigōng grandfather
(on mother's side)
wàipó grandmother
(on mother's side)
wàn 10,000
wǎn evening, night
wǎn'ān goodnight
wǎng towards
wǎngbā internet café
wǎngfǎn return journey

wǎnshang evening

wǎnshang hǎo good evening

wèi measure word; hello on the phone

Wēi'ěrshì Wales

Wēi'ěrshìrén Welsh (person)

wéijīn scarf

wēishìjì whisky

wō nest

wǒ I; me

wò lie

wǒde my; mine

wǒmen we; us

wū house

wǔ five

wūlóng chá oolong tea

wǔshí fifty

X

xī west

xiā shrimp

xià next

xiànchāo jī cash machine

xiǎng want; think about

xiāngbīn champagne

xiāngcài Hunan cuisine

Xiānggǎng Hong Kong

Xiānggǎngrén Hong Kong person

xiāngjiāo banana

xiàngliàn necklace

xiānsheng sir, Mr

xiànzài now

xiǎo small; young

xiǎojie Miss

xiǎomàibù corner shop

xiǎoshí hour

xiàwǔ afternoon

xià yī tàng next train or bus

Xībānyá Spain

Xībānyáwén Spanish (language)

Xībānyáyǔ Spanish (language)

xībiān West

xīcānguǎn Western food restaurant

xièxie thank, thank you

xī guā watermelon

xīhóngshì tomato

xǐhuan like

xìng surname

xīngjí star rating

xíngli luggage

xīngqī week

xīngqī'èr Tuesday

xīngqīliù Saturday

xīngqīsān Wednesday

xīngqīsì Thursday

xīngqītiān Sunday

xīngqīwǔ Friday

xīngqīyī Monday

Xīní Sydney

Xīnjiāpō Singapore

Xīnxīlánrén New Zealander

xìnyòngkǎ credit card

xǐyīfáng laundrette

xué to learn, to study

xuésheng student

xuéyuàn college

Y

yā duck

yángróng cashmere

yángròu lamb

yángtáo starfruit

yánsè colour

yāo one

yào to want, need

yàoshi key

yě also

yéye grandfather (on father's side)

yēzi coconut

yī one

yī bǎi hundred

yībiàn once

Yìdàlìrén Italian (person)

Yìdàlìwén Italian (language)

yìdiǎn a little bit

yīgòng altogether

Yíhéyuán the Summer Palace

yí kè a quarter, 15 minutes

yí lù píng ān bon voyage

Yìndùníxīyà Indonesia

Yīnggélán UK

Yīnggélánrén British (person)

Yīngguórén British (person)

yīngtáo cherry

Yīngwén English (language)

Yīngyǔ English (language)

yìngwò hard sleeper

yìngzuò hard seat

yínháng bank

yīnyuètīng music hall

yīshēng doctor

yíxià a little (used after a verb)

yīyàng the same

yīyuàn hospital

yīyuè January

yìzhí straight, along

yòng use

Yōnghégōng Yonghe Palace (a Tibetan Buddhist temple)

yǒu to have

yòu again; right

yóujú post office

yóumèn braised

yóupiào stamp

yóuyǒngchí swimming pool

yú fish

yǔ rain

yù jade

yuán unit of currency

yuǎn far

yùdìng to reserve

yuè month

yuècài Cantonese cuisine

Yuènán Vietnam

yùshì bathroom

Z

zài in, on, at; again
zàijiàn goodbye
zǎocān breakfast
zǎoshang morning
zǎoshang hǎo good morning
zěnme how
zěnmeyàng how; how about it?; how are you?
zhá deep fried
zhāng *measure word*
zhàngdān bill
zhàngfu husband
zhǎnlǎnhuì exhibition
zhànpiào standing (ticket)
zhǎo look for, find
zhāodàisuǒ economy guest houses
zhàopiàn photo

zhè this
zhècài Zhejiang cuisine
zhēn really; real, true
zhēnsī pure silk
zhēnzhū pearl
zhèr here
zhèxiē these
zhǐ only
zhīdao know
zhídào until
zhíyè profession
zhōng middle
Zhōngcān Chinese cuisine
Zhōngguó China
Zhōngguórén Chinese (person)
Zhōngguó Tiělù China Rail
Zhōngwén Chinese (language)

zhōngxīn centre
zhōu provincial capital
zhōumò weekend
zhù live, stay
zhǔcài main course
zhǔrèn director
zhūròu pork
zhǔshí staple carbohydrate
zhǔxí chairperson
zhǔyi idea
zìxíngchē bicycle
zǒu walk
zǒulù walk, on foot
zuìdī jià lowest price
zuìjìn recently; nearest
zuò sit; do
zuǒ left
zuǒ biān left side

English–Chinese glossary

A

able: be able to, can néng
accountant kuàijìshī
afternoon xiàwǔ
again yòu; zài
air-conditioning kōngtiáo
all dōu
allow ràng
along yìzhí
also yě
altogether yīgòng
America Měiguó
American (person) Měiguórén
and hé
apartment gōngyù
apple píngguǒ
arrive dào
art gallery huàláng
arts and crafts shop gōngyì měishù diàn
at zài
Australia Àodàlìyà
Australian Àodàlìyàrén
automobile qìchē

B

banana xiāngjiāo
bank yínháng
bathroom yùshì
be: am, is, are shì
beancurd dòufu
beansprout dòuyá
beautiful piàoliang
beef niúròu
beer píjiǔ
Beijing person Běijīngrén
bicycle zìxíngchē
big dà
bill zhàngdān; settle the bill jiézhàng
black hēi(sè)
black tea hóng chá
blue lán(sè)

boiled (lit. white) rice bái (mǐ)fàn
bon voyage yí lù píng ān
born: be born shēng
both dōu
bottle píng
boyfriend nán péngyou
braised yóumèn
brandy báilándì
breakfast zǎocān
British (person) Yīngguórén, Yīnggélánrén
bureau jú
bus gōnggòng qìchē
bus stop chēzhàn
business card míngpiàn
but dànshì
buy mǎi

C

café kāfēiguǎn
call: be called jiào
can, be able to huì, néng
can, may kěyǐ
can, tin guàn
Canadian Jiānádàrén
Canberra Kānpéilā
Cantonese cuisine yuècài
cap màozi
cappuccino kǎbùqínuò
car chē
cash machine xiànchāo jī
cashmere yángróng
centre zhōngxīn
chairperson zhǔxí
champagne xiāngbīn
cheap piányi
Cheers! gān bēi
cherry yīngtáo
chicken jī
chicken (meat) jī(ròu)
child háizi
China Rail Zhōngguó Tiělù

China Zhōngguó
Chinese (person) Zhōngguórén;
(language) Zhōngwén
Chinese broccoli jièlán
Chinese cuisine Zhōngcān
Chinese leaves báicài
chocolate qiǎokèlì
chopsticks kuàizi
chrysanthemum tea júhuā chá
city (chéng) shì
close guānmén
clothes fúzhuāng
coconut yēzi
coffee kāfēi
cola kělè
colleague tóngshì
college xuéyuàn
colour yánsè
come lái
company gōngsī
connection point jiēkǒu
contain hán, bāo
corner shop xiǎomàibù
correct duì
country guó; guójiā
countryside nóngcūn
credit card xìnyòngkǎ
crossroad lùkǒu
cup bēi
curry gālí

D

date hào
daughter nǚ'ér
day tiān
death sǐ
December shí'èryuè
deep fried zhá
delicious (for drink) hǎohē; (for food) hǎochī
department store bǎihuò

shāngdiàn
destination mùdìdì
die sǐ
director zhǔrèn
dish cài
divorce líhūn
do zuò
doctor yīshēng
double room shuāngrén
fángjiān
downstairs lóuxià
drink hē
duck yā; roast duck
kǎoyā
dumpling jiǎozi

E
earring ěrhuán
east dōng
eat chī
egg dàn, jīdàn
eight bā
eighty bāshí
elder brother gēge
elder sister jiějie
engineer gōngchéngshī
English (language)
Yīngwén, Yīngyǔ
enjoy your meal
mànmàn chī
enough gòu
enter jìn
even gèng
evening wǎn, wǎnshang
everyday měi tiān
exhibition zhǎnlǎnhuì
expensive guì
extra large jiā dà
extremely fēicháng
extremely tài

F
factory gōngchǎng
family jiā
family jiātíng
family member jiārén
far yuǎn
father bàba

February èryuè
female nǚ
fifty wǔshí
find zhǎo
fish yú
five wǔ
flat, apartment gōngyù
floor (level) céng
follow gēn
food fàncài
foot: on foot zǒulù
for gěi
Forbidden City Gùgōng
fork chāzi
form biǎo
forty sìshí
four sì
France Fǎguó
French (language)
Fǎwén, Fǎyǔ
French person Fǎguórén
Friday xīngqīwǔ
fried jiān
fried noodles chǎomiàn
fried rice chǎofàn
friend péngyou
from cóng
full mǎn; be full chībǎo

G
garden huāyuán
garlic suàn
German (language)
Déwén; (nationality)
Déguórén
Germany Déguó
get to know a person
rènshi
girlfriend nǚ péngyou
give gěi
glass bēi
go qù
good hǎo
good evening wǎnshang
hǎo
good morning zǎoshang
hǎo
goodbye zàijiàn

goodnight wǎn'ān
goose é
grandfather (on father's
side) yéye; (on mother's
side) wàigōng
grandmother (on father's
side) nǎinai; (on mother's
side) wàipó
Great Wall Chángchéng
green lǜ(sè); green tea
lǜ chá; green vegetables
qīngcài
greengrocer's shuǐguǒ
diàn
guest house (economy)
zhāodàisuǒ
gym jiànshēngfáng

H
half bàn
hamburger hànbǎo bāo
handbag shǒutíbāo
happy gāoxìng
hard seat yìngzuò
hard sleeper yìngwò
hat màozi
have yǒu; don't have méi
yǒu; have to bìxū
have a look kànkan
have a try shìshi
he tā
hello nǐ hǎo; (formal) nín
hǎo; on the phone wèi
help bāngzhù
her tā
here zhèr
him tā
holiday: on holiday dùjià
Hong Kong Xiānggǎng;
Hong Kong person
Xiānggǎngrén
hospital yīyuàn
hot and sour suānlà
hotel fàndiàn, bīnguǎn,
jiǔdiàn
hour xiǎoshí
house wū
how long? duō jiǔ?

how many?, how much? duōshao?
how old duōdà?; jǐ suì?
how? zěnme?; How about it?; How are you? zěnmeyàng?
hundred bǎi
hungry è
husband zhàngfu

I

I wǒ
ice bīng
idea zhǔyi
in zài
in addition hái
in that case nàme
include hán, bāo
Indonesia Yìndùníxīyà
internet café wǎngbā
internet hùliánwǎng
introduce jièshào
invite qǐng
Ireland Ài'ěrlán
Italian (language) Yìdàlìwén; (person) Yìdàlìrén

J

jacket shàngyī
jade yù
January yīyuè
Japan Rìběn
Japanese (language) Rìwén, Rìyǔ; (person) Rìběnrén
jasmine tea huā chá
job gōngzuò
journalist jìzhě
just a minute shāo děng

K

key yàoshi
kilometre gōnglǐ
kite fēngzheng
know zhīdao; get to know a person rènshi
Korean (person) Hánguórén

L

lake hú
lamb yángròu
Lancaster Lánkǎisītè
landscape painting shānshuǐhuà
large size dà hào
later hòulái
laundrette xǐyīfáng
lawyer lǜshī
learn xué
leather pígé
leave kāi
left zuǒ; left side zuǒ biān
lemon níngméng
library túshūguǎn
lie wò
lift, escalator diàntī
like xǐhuan
little (a little) (with a verb) yíxià; a little (bit) yìdiǎn; (few) shǎo
live zhù
lobster lóngxiā
local (person) běndìrén
London Lúndūn
look kàn; have a look kànkan
look for zhǎo
lost: be lost mí lù
lowest price zuìdī jià
luggage xíngli
luxury háohuá
lychee lìzhī

M

madam nǚshì
main course zhǔcài
Malaysia Mǎláixīyà
male nán
manager jīnglǐ
mango mángguǒ
many duō, hěnduō
map dìtú
marine sauce, gravy lǔshuǐ
marjong májiàng
market shìchǎng

married jiéhūn
martial art gōngfu
may kěyǐ; may I ask? qǐng wèn?
me wǒ
meal fàn
meat ròu
meet jiàn
melon guā
menu càidān
middle zhōng
milk niúnǎi
mine wǒde
mineral water kuàngquán shuǐ
minute fēnzhōng; just a minute shāo děng
Miss xiǎojie
mobile phone shǒujī
Monday xīngqīyī
money qián
month yuè
more gèng
morning shàngwǔ, zǎoshang
mother māma
motorbike mótuōchē
mountain shān
Mr xiānsheng
Mrs tàitai
museum bówùguǎn
mushroom mógu
music hall yīnyuètīng
must bìxū
my wǒde

N

name míngzi
name card míngpiàn
nationality guójí
nearby fùjìn
nearest zuìjìn
necklace xiàngliàn
need yào
nest wō
New York Niǔyuē
New Zealander Xīnxīlánrén
next xià; next to

pángbiān; next bus xià yī
tàng (gōnggòng qìchē);
next train xià yī tàng
(huǒchē)
night wǎn
nine jiǔ
ninety jiǔshí
noisy chǎo
noodles miàn(tiáo)
north běi
not bù; not at all nǎli nǎli
November shíyīyuè
now xiànzài
number hào, hàomǎ;
phone number diànhuà
hàomǎ
nut guǒrén

O

o'clock diǎn
of course dāngrán
office bàngōngshì
on zài; on foot zǒulù
once yībiàn
one yāo, yī
onion cōng
only zhǐ
oolong tea wūlóng chá
open kāi, kāimén
opera house gējùyuàn
opposite duìmiàn
or háishi, huòzhě
orange chéngzi
orange juice júzi zhī
order a meal diǎncài
other biéde, qítā
over there nàbiān

P

packet bāo
park gōngyuán
partner àiren
pashmina, shawl pījiān
passport hùzhào
pay fù
peach táozi
pear lízi

pearl zhēnzhū
person rén
Phillipines Fēilǜbīn
phone diànhuà; phone
number diànhuà hàomǎ
photo zhàopiàn
pineapple bōluó
pizza bǐsà bǐng
please qǐng
porcelain táocí
pork zhūròu
post office yóujú
postcard míngxìnpiàn
prawn dàxiā
present: be present
guānglín
profession zhíyè
province shěng
public gōnggòng
pure silk zhēnsī
pure wool chúnmáo

Q

quarter (a quarter), 15
minutes yī kè; (a) quarter
to chà yī kè
question word ma

R

rain yǔ
real zhēn
really zhēn
recently zuìjìn
red hóng(sè)
red wine hóng pútáojiǔ
reserve yùdìng
restaurant fànguǎn,
cānguǎn
return journey wǎngfǎn
rice mǐfàn; rice wine
mǐjiǔ
right (direction) yòu
river hé
RMB (Chinese currency)
Rénmínbì
road lù
roast duck kǎoyā

roasted kǎo
room fángjiān
route lù

S

safe (box) bǎoxiǎnxiāng
same yíyàng
Saturday xīngqīliù
say shuō
scarf wéijīn
Scotland Sūgélán
Scottish (person)
Sūgélánrén
sea hǎi
seafood hǎixiān
seaside hǎibiān
seat: hard seat yìngzuò;
soft seat ruǎnzuò
see you later huí jiàn
sell mài
September jiǔyuè
settle the bill jiézhàng
seven qī
seventy qīshí
she tā
shirt chènshān
shop shāngdiàn
shopping centre gòuwù
zhōngxīn
shrimp xiā
side biān
silk sī; pure silk zhēnsī
Singapore Xīnjiāpō
single (unmarried)
dānshēn
single journey dānchéng
single room dānjiān,
dānrén fángjiān
sir xiānsheng
sit zuò
six liù
sixty liùshí
size hào
sliced beef niúliù
slow màn
small xiǎo
soft seat ruǎnzuò
soft sleeper ruǎnwò

son érzi
sorry duìbuqǐ
so-so mǎmǎhūhū
soup tāng
south nán
South Korea Hánguó
Spain Xībānyá
Spanish (language)
Xībānyáwén, Xībānyáyǔ
spare ribs páigǔ
speak shuō
spicy (hot) là
spinach bōcài
spoon sháozi
spouse àiren
stamp yóupiào
standing (ticket)
zhànpiào
star rating xīngjí
starfruit yángtáo
stay zhù
steamed qīngzhēng
steamed bun bāozi
stewed in dark soy sauce
hóngshāo
still hái
stir fry chǎo
straight yìzhí
student xuésheng
study xué
suburb jiāoqū
sugar táng
Summer Palace Yíhéyuán
suncream fángshàiyóu
Sunday xīngqītiān
super chāojí
supermarket chāojí
shìchǎng
surname guìxìng, xìng
sweet and sour tángcù
swimming pool
yóuyǒngchí
Sydney Xīní

T
t'ai chi tàijí
tangerine júzi

taxi chūzūchē
tea chá; nǎi chá
teach jiāo
teacher lǎoshī
telephone diànhuà
ten shí
ten thousand yí wàn
Thailand Tàiguó
thank you xièxie nǐ
thanks xièxie
that nà
their tāmende
theirs tāmende
them tāmen
then nàme
there nà
these zhèxiē
they tāmen
thick hòu
think about xiǎng
thirty sānshí
this zhè
thousand qiān
three sān
Thursday xīngqīsì
ticket piào
ticket office shòupiàochù
tie lǐngdài
time shíhou
today jīntiān
toilet cèsuǒ
tomato xīhóngshì
tomorrow míngtiān
tonight jīnwǎn
too tài
tour lǚyóu
tour guide dǎoyóu
tourist board lǚyóujú
towards wǎng
town centre shì zhōngxīn
traffic light hónglǜdēng
train station huǒchēzhàn
travel lǚyóu
travel agent lǚxíngshè
treat (somebody to a
meal) qǐngkè
true zhēn

try shì; try on, have a try
shìshi
Tuesday xīngqī'èr
turn guǎi
twenty èrshí
twin room liǎngrén
fángjiān
two èr, liǎng

U
UK Yīnggélán
underground dìtiě
understand dǒng
university dàxué
until zhídào
upstairs lóushàng
us wǒmen
use yòng

V
vacant kòng
vegetable: seasonal
vegetable shícài
vegetarian sù, chīsù;
vegetarian dish sùcài
vehicle chē
very hěn, fēicháng
Vietnam Yuènán

W
wait děng
waiter fúwùyuán
waitress fúwùyuán
wake up jiàoxǐng
Wales Wēi'ěrshì
walk zǒu, zǒulù
want yào, xiǎng
water shuǐ
watermelon xī guā
we wǒmen
Wednesday xīngqīsān
week xīngqī
weekend zhōumò
welcome huānyíng,
huānyíng guānglín
well hǎo

Welsh (person)
Wēi'ěrshìrén
west xī; West xībiān
Western food restaurant
xīcānguǎn
what? shénme?; what
number/what date?
jǐhào?; What nationality
are you? Nǎ guó rén?
when? shénme shíhou?
where? nali?, nǎr?
which? nǎ?
whisky wēishìjì
white bái(sè)
white wine bái pútáojiǔ
wife, Mrs tàitai

wind fēng
wine jiǔ, pútáojiǔ; white
wine bái pútáojiǔ; wine
bar jiǔbā
with dài, gēn
wool yángmáo
work gōngzuò
workmate tóngshì
worship bài

Y
year nián
years old suì; (used when
asking old people their
age) suìshu
yellow huáng(sè)

yes shìde
you nǐ, (formal singular)
nín, (plural) nǐmen
you're welcome bú kèqi,
bú xiè
young xiǎo
younger brother dìdi
younger sister mèimei
your nǐde
yours nǐde
youth hostel qīngnián
lǚshè

Z
zero líng
Zhejiang cuisine zhècài